"Indulging in the world of mushrooms has never been more delicious and delightful than with this exceptional cookbook. Clear and concise instructions, meticulous detailing of more than twenty mushroom species, and a vast array of globally-inspired recipes will thrill both novices and seasoned chefs alike. It is a testament to the author's passion for mushrooms and their vast culinary potential, and not only is it a comprehensive guide, it's a visual feast as well. I can't wait to get cooking!"

—CYNTHIA GRAUBART, JAMES BEARD AWARD–WINNING COOKBOOK AUTHOR OF FOURTEEN COOKBOOKS, COOKING TEACHER, AND CULINARY TELEVISION PRODUCER

"This book is a love letter to those of us who are passionate about foraging and creating good food with our mushrooms, and should be required reading for anyone who delights in what's out there, in the forests and meadows, awaiting the curious—and hungry—forager."

—BRITT BUNYARD, PHD, NOTED LECTURER, AUTHOR, MYCOLOGIST, AND FOUNDER AND EDITOR-IN-CHIEF OF *FUNGI MAGAZINE*

"There is a recipe for everyone in this lovely book (I'm going for Maitake Philly Cheesesteak). *Mushroom Gastronomy* is a welcome addition to the library of anyone who loves mushrooms!"

—EUGENIA BONE, CHEF, INTERNATIONALLY KNOWN FOOD AND SCIENCE WRITER, AND AUTHOR OF THE JAMES BEARD AWARD–NOMINATED COOKBOOK *WELL PRESERVED*

"This cookbook is a celebration of mushrooms. The recipes are approachable yet adventurous, making it perfect for both beginners and seasoned chefs. As mushrooms—particularly wild varieties—continue gaining popularity, Krista's book offers valuable guidance to those exploring the unique culinary potential of mushrooms."

—JACK HAMRICK, COFOUNDER AND CEO OF FORAGED—A MARKETPLACE FOR WILD AND SPECIALTY FOODS

"Krista Town's expert knowledge and indispensable guidance will help you navigate the incredible world of mushrooms and fungi. Her new book is the ultimate culinary resource for both foraged and cultivated varieties, with recipes that are sure to inspire even the most ardent mycophiles."

—RAY SHEEHAN, RESTAURATEUR, MULTI AWARD-WINNING CHEF, AND COOKBOOK AUTHOR

# MUSHROOM
## GASTRONOMY

KRISTA TOWNS

Gibbs Smith

First Edition

28  27  26  25  24      5  4  3  2  1

Text © 2024 Krista Towns

Photographs © 2024 Krista Towns

Published by

Gibbs Smith

P.O. Box 667

Layton, Utah 84041

1.800.835.4993 orders

www.gibbs-smith.com

Designed by Rita Sowins | Sowins Design and Ryan Thomann

Production Design by Renee Bond

Printed and bound in China

Gibbs Smith books are printed on either recycled, 100% post-consumer waste, FSC-certified papers or on paper produced from sustainable PEFC-certified forest/controlled wood source. Learn more at www.pefc.org.

Library of Congress Control Number: 2023942679

ISBN: 978-1-4236-6497-0

PUBLISHER'S DISCLAIMER: This book is not a foraging identification guide. It is the reader's responsibility to ensure they have accurately identified any mushroom before consuming it. The author and publisher disclaim all responsibility of allergy, injury, illness, or death resulting from touching, gathering, or ingesting, in any form, the mushrooms listed in this book. Readers assume all legal responsibility for their actions. Information provided in this book is not intended to diagnose, prescribe, or treat any illness. Please consult your physician for personalized medical advice, and always seek the advice of a physician or other qualified healthcare provider with any questions regarding a medical condition.

Printed in China using  FSC® Certified materials

# CONTENTS

# FOREWORD

**KRISTA AND I SHARE** a personal history with the South and a love for its richly vibrant cuisine. I'm thrilled her new cookbook, *Mushroom Gastronomy*, includes recipes with twists on Southern-style dishes using mushrooms like Baked Corn and Cheddar Grits with Wild Mushroom Ragu and Reishi Raspberry Tea.

*Mushroom Gastronomy* introduces us to a variety of mushrooms through familiar classic-style recipes. Filled with extensive tips on selecting, storing, and cooking with mushrooms, it's an incredible guide to help us navigate through the less familiar types of mushrooms popping up at grocery stores, farmers' markets, and even in supplements at the pharmacy.

With my health and wellness journey, I've embraced that mushrooms are a delicious addition to our diets. They are good plant-forward meat replacements, and highly effective functional foods with tremendous health benefits for our brain and nervous systems. And reducing the consumption of meat by adding mushrooms to our meals is not just a healthy personal choice, but also helps reduce our carbon footprint.

Multiple companies around the world are developing innovative fungal solutions to combat toxic waste spills, pest control, and disease. The *Smithsonian Magazine* recently reported that mushrooms may communicate with one another using electrical impulses! Scientific research tells us some mushrooms can potentially prevent age-related dementia. It seems there is nothing that mushrooms cannot do—giving a whole new meaning to the term "magic mushrooms."

Read on for an incredible selection of good-for-you recipes, helpful tips, and insight written by a mushroom expert and an accomplished cook who has devoted years to studying, refining recipes, and pairing flavors with these fascinating fungi.

Bon Appetit, Y'all!

**VIRGINIA WILLIS**, Chef, James Beard Award winner,
television producer, and food writer

6

# ACKNOWLEDGMENTS

**I DEEPLY APPRECIATE** all of you who have helped me along the way in creating this book. As a first-time cookbook author, I had little idea of the amount of work involved in putting a book together. The long, arduous process is daunting and thrives on the encouragement given by friends and family, with untiring efforts from agents, editors, and publishers. Much like the mycelium underneath our feet and under every mushroom, cells repeatedly branching while building a vast network of support, you have helped turn my vision into a tangible thing, a handheld book to be read, shared, and enjoyed.

A special thank you to my editor, Michelle Branson, and the amazing teams at Gibbs Smith; Renee Bond, Rita Sowins, and Ryan Thomann, who did such a beautiful job with the design and layout of this book, Michelle Bayuk and the marketing team; Moneka Hewlett, Kellie Robles, Paulina Siparsky, and Heather Scott who are working hard promoting the heck out of it.

To my agents, Kathryn Williams and Sam Hiyate at The Rights Factory, the infamous "Professor" Britt Bunyard, founder of *Fungi Magazine* who's been a wonderful mentor and friend, Jan Hammond (plays a mean dulcimer and always makes my articles look terrific), talented chefs and authors Cynthia Graubart and Ray Sheehan for your much appreciated advice. Thank you to George Weinstein at the Atlanta Writers Conference, Ursula Dodge and Eric Gum for kindly letting us take photos at their gorgeous farm, The Vinegar Works, and dear friends Hector Lahera and Ben Crawford of Circular Farm.

Thank you to Regalis Foods for sourcing the most unique strains of mushrooms available with consistent quality and beauty, Jack and Andy of Foraged Market for providing a valuable resource for fresh foraged mushrooms, and Field and Forest and North Spore for their prolific growing kits and supplies.

For uplifting inspiration, thanks to David Byrne and Arbutus/Reasons to be Cheerful, and Paul Stamets and his wonderful film, *Fantastic Fungi*.

My thanks to the many mushroom enthusiasts who have encouraged and assisted me on this journey. For Zela and Kerby who always make me smile. And finally for my amazing husband, John, who has been my constant source of support. It is my greatest joy to spend my life with you.

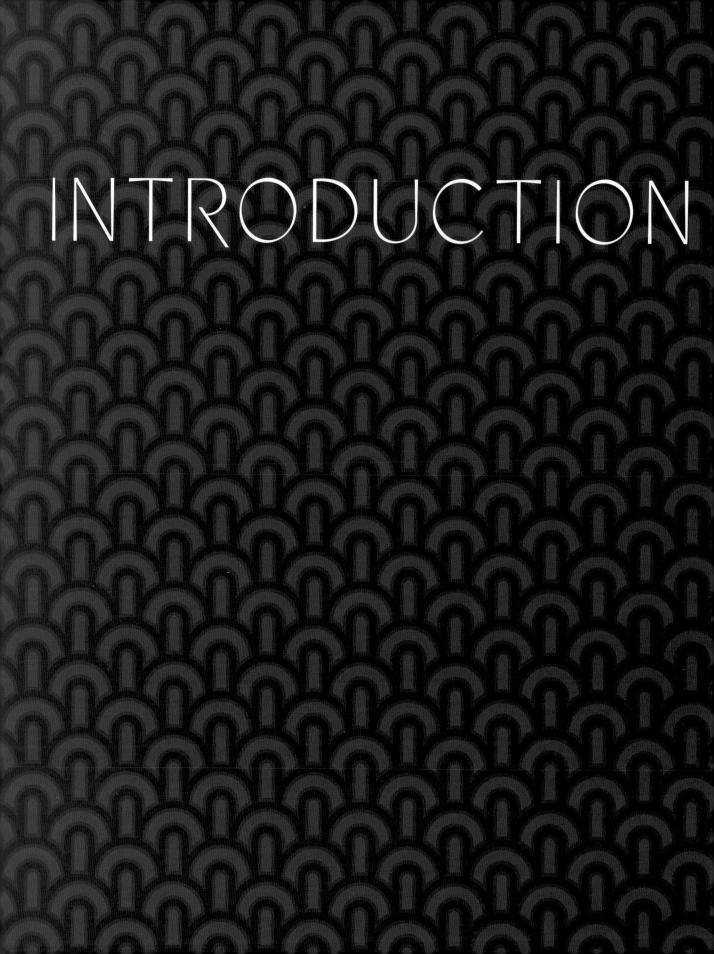

# INTRODUCTION

**IF YOU'RE READING THIS BOOK,** you're likely passionate about cooking and may be curious about the new mushroom varieties popping up in your local grocery. You might be concerned about the environment and committed to reducing your meat consumption or have been reading about the health benefits that mushrooms offer. But then what's next? What mushroom variety will work best with the dish or recipes you have in mind? How will you prepare and store them? I'm hoping to introduce you to mushrooms you aren't already familiar with, answer many of your questions, and help you feel more at ease cooking with them.

I've always loved mushrooms (once I'd tasted them fresh), and over the years, I sourced and cooked with as many varieties as I could find. My passion likely stems from adventures roaming the woods as a child growing up in rural Ohio. Much to the frustration of my well-meaning parents, I loved dirt and the tiny plants that grew from it, quickly shunned baby dolls and Barbies, and preferred instead to roam the woods. I chewed on wild licorice, snacked on blackberries, and bravely swung from large oak tree limbs. My explorations turned into day-long adventures.

I came to cooking later, it was a satisfying retreat from school and work, and something that I enjoyed without ever a thought to making it part of a career. I attended local classes with chefs here and in France, and as I gained skill and confidence over the years, began catering private and then public events, and eventually entered cooking competitions—evolving to developing recipes, food styling, photography, and food writing. Through a twist of fate, I met and began working with a local couple who owned a successful mushroom farm, and I was able to experience the joy of cultivating mushrooms, waking to their overnight growth, each at their own pace, with their unique beauty and flavor. I've also enjoyed the thrill of stumbling upon an elusive patch of morels or spotting a cluster of oyster mushrooms at the end of a long day foraging in the woods. I realize some people have hesitations toward cooking with or eating mushrooms, especially with the wide varieties now available. Overcoming tentativeness through easy to prepare, familiar, and delicious recipes became my motivation to write this book.

# ABOUT THE RECIPES

Having the opportunity to cook with a variety of mushrooms is an indulgence and a pleasure. Mushrooms are fascinating and delicious; cultured or wild. In this cookbook, I've included recipes inspired by nationalities that embrace mushrooms. Spain, Italy, France, and Asia being the most common. In these countries, mushrooms are abundant and revered throughout their history, both through cultivation and foraging. And they are masterfully included in their local cuisines.

My challenge and joy is in matching each variety with cooking techniques and flavors that showcase the best of their culinary qualities. While creating these recipes, my intent was to allow the mushrooms to tell their own stories; smoky maitake mushrooms, with their dense texture and meaty flavor, are wonderful on the barbecue, either grilled or smoked, with a light marinade of lemon, olive oil, and garlic. The earthiness of shiitakes makes them perfect for a rich ragu, while lion's mane, with its delicate seafood-like flavor and shreddable texture is perfect for crab cakes, egg rolls, and any light pasta dish.

Cooking shouldn't depend on exotic or expensive ingredients. Often the best dishes come out of a simple, well-stocked kitchen, prepared with a little effort and a touch of inspiration. You should be able to make most of these recipes with ingredients you already have on hand or those that are available with a quick trip to the local grocery store. Make good use of your kitchen tools, especially the scale. Mushrooms vary in weight; a scale will give you the correct amounts you'll need for a recipe without guessing.

Feel free to substitute; the recipes are meant to be used as much for inspiration as instruction. Your result may be a little different but equally or even more delicious. Hopefully along the way you will find your own voice and have fun creating dishes that will best suit your desires while including this special ingredient in your cooking.

LEARN HOW TO COOK,
TRY NEW RECIPES,
LEARN FROM YOUR MISTAKES,
BE FEARLESS
AND ABOVE ALL, HAVE FUN.
—JULIA CHILD

# SAFETY WITH MUSHROOMS

- Never consume any foraged mushrooms until you are 100 percent sure they are safe to consume. If unsure, take a pass!
- If you are not an experienced forager, have an expert confirm the mushroom's identity and safety.
- All wild mushrooms must be cooked before eating.
- When trying any new mushroom, consume it in very small amounts first to determine if you may have an adverse reaction.
- Never eat mushrooms with a slimy texture, signs of mold, or those past their prime.
- Please consult with your doctor before consuming any mushroom for medicinal purposes, especially if you already take medications.

## RAW MUSHROOMS

Sliced, raw cultivated mushrooms are often served in salads and offered in salad bars in restaurants—usually white buttons. These, along with beech, cremini, and portobellos, are likely safe to consume raw. In general, though, it is wise to cook your mushrooms before eating them, and there are a few reasons:

- When you eat a mushroom raw, the nutrients are not as easily digestible. Mushrooms contain chitin, a nearly indigestible compound that keeps the essential nutrients in raw mushrooms from being absorbed. To release their nutrients, they must be cooked.
- All other mushrooms, especially foraged mushrooms, must be cooked before eating. They have a higher potential to contain bacteria that can cause food poisoning. Morels are an example of a wild mushroom that should never be consumed raw. Even undercooked shiitakes can cause an allergic reaction due to their lentinan content.
- And besides, cooked mushrooms taste better!

# THE MUSHROOM PANTRY

This chapter should help you set up your pantry with mushroom-friendly ingredients to have on hand for creating your best dishes. Select your basics and build from there as you continue to cook with mushrooms and experiment with new varieties and preparations.

## OILS AND FATS

### AVOCADO OIL

Produced from the pulp of (ideally) organic avocados, this oil is rich in monounsaturated fats and other essential nutrients. A high smoke point makes it versatile and safe for medium- to high-heat cooking, grilling, stir-frying, baking, or broiling.

### BUTTER

A simply delicious ingredient that will enhance most anything, butter is wonderful with mushrooms! Buy unsalted, always check the sell-by date, and ensure it comes from a high-quality producer and is made ideally from organically farmed, grass-fed cows. Butter from grass-fed cows contains higher levels of vitamin K and other nutrients than butter from grain-fed cows. Store extra portions in the freezer so you will always have a good quality product on hand. Use it to sauté or to make flavorful mushroom butters; a delicious addition to grilled vegetables or meats. Milk solids can cause foods to burn, so either mix butter with oil when high-heat sautéing or make clarified butter, or ghee. To make clarified butter, simply melt unsalted butter in a saucepan over medium-low heat, skim the foam, and strain the solids. Store in a sealed glass container. Both clarified butter and ghee are fantastic for pan-sautéing or -frying, and may be used instead of butter, oil, or a combination of butter and oil, in any recipe in this book.

Ghee is heated for a longer period and has a nuttier flavor and a deeper color than clarified butter. To make ghee, melt unsalted butter in a small heavy saucepan over very low heat, and skim off foam that floats to the top as it cooks. Continue to cook slowly, stirring occasionally until reduced by 25 percent, about 45 minutes to an hour. At this point the milk solids will have turned golden brown and settled to the bottom of the saucepan. Strain and transfer to a glass, sealable jar.

Both clarified butter and ghee will store in the pantry for up to three months, in the refrigerator for up to a year, and in the freezer indefinitely. **TIP:** Add spices like ginger or cumin to the ghee at the beginning of the cooking process for added flavor.

## CANOLA OIL

A popular, neutral-flavored oil with a moderately high smoke point, good for sautéing.

## COCONUT OIL

I love using virgin or unrefined coconut oil for low to medium heat, sautéing mushrooms and vegetables, or in marinades for Southeast Asian and Indian dishes. The flavor is subtle, but it adds a light tropical aroma and a hint of vanilla-coconut flavor. It is not suitable for frying.

Refined coconut oil has little flavor and a higher smoking point, so it is acceptable for high-heat stir-frying.

Due to the oil's high fat content, you may want to use 25 percent less coconut oil or

even more than that compared to butter or other oils.

Store coconut oil in a cool, dark location in a sealed container or in the refrigerator.

## DUCK FAT

This is one of the most delicious fats you can use when searing or pan-roasting just about anything. It's classically paired with potatoes, and is equally good for sautéing or roasting mushrooms.

It's also a reasonably healthy fat, containing higher levels of oleic acid and monounsaturated and polyunsaturated fats than butter and high levels of amino acids. It has more saturated fat than olive oil but is a healthier alternative to butter.

Store, refrigerated, for a few months, or freeze.

## LEAF LARD

Leaf lard is the choicest lard available. Made from a leaf-shaped portion of fat around the kidneys, leaf lard is softer and creamier than other types of lard. It is prized for its smooth consistency, mild flavor, and a high smoking point, making it ideal for frying and searing. Consider using this type of rendered fat for a super-flaky pie crust or pastry.

## OLIVE OIL

An essential staple to have in your pantry, olive oil is not only a super-healthy oil, but also one of the very best for cooking. Olive oil contains vitamin E and many powerful antioxidants, which give numerous health benefits. It has been named "the healthiest fat on earth," partly because of its unique ability to reduce the risk of heart disease. The oil's smoke point is around 375 to 405 degrees F, making it a good choice for most cooking methods, including pan-searing and frying. Have two kinds in your pantry; a less expensive, mild but good quality, extra-virgin one for cooking and dressings, and if in the budget, indulge in a high quality extra-virgin olive oil for an additional final drizzle to your mushroom dishes.

## PEANUT OIL

This is my personal favorite for frying. While peanut oil has a slightly nutty flavor, it's generally a good, neutral option for most recipes. It has a high smoke point (around 450 degrees F), so can withstand high temperatures without burning. Peanut oil is rich in vitamin E, offering protective benefits against chronic disease.

## SESAME OIL

A must-have, versatile oil for your pantry. Both light and toasted varieties are popular in Middle Eastern, Chinese, Japanese, Korean, and South Indian cuisines. A small amount goes a long way when added to a dish, but it is delicious and holds up well in a stir-fry due to its high smoke point. Add a few teaspoons to your frying oil when making tempura to add extra sesame flavor.

## SOYBEAN OIL

This oil is another good choice for frying due to its neutral flavor and high smoke point.

## WALNUT OIL

Walnuts and walnut oil pair nicely with mushrooms, and like other healthy oils, they are rich in both nutrients and antioxidants. Walnut oil has a low smoke point and a nice nutty flavor. It's a terrific choice for salad dressings, for drizzling on grilled or roasted mushrooms, or to use as a finishing touch to a mushroom risotto or bisque.

# DRIED MUSHROOMS

At some point, you may find yourself with more mushrooms than you know what to do with. The solution is to dry your extras and store them for up to a year.

If you don't have any on hand for a recipe, you will likely find a wide range of varieties available in your local market. If you're only choosing one, then pick the porcini! A little bit goes a long way, and its deep, smoky, umami flavor adds depth to almost any savory dish.

Make powders from your dried mushrooms by grinding them in a spice grinder and keep them in a small jar for adding to butters or use as a rub to coat roasts or steaks.

# PASTA

No pantry is complete without a stash of dried pasta. Long or short, tubes or curly, all are great to have on hand to pull together a quick meal.

The better Italian-style dried pasta, usually made in Italy, is worth the extra dollar or two. These pastas are cut using bronze dies, and the texture is far better than the less expensive brands offered on most grocery store shelves. You'll find them in upscale grocers and online. If you enjoy Asian-style dishes, include ramen, soba, and thin vermicelli.

# SALTS

The irreplaceable salt! Coarse salt, sea salt, and smoked salts are good for cooking mushrooms and pretty much any foods. Use regular sea salt or kosher salt for cooking and add the flaky sea salts to roasts and the specialty sea salts to finish. Maldon is a premier large, flaked sea

Diamond Crystal kosher salt is easy to pinch and sprinkle with, and contains less sodium than table salt, making it more difficult to oversalt your food. The recipes in this book were made using Diamond Crystal kosher salt unless otherwise specified.

## SOY SAUCES

Salty and sweet, and all made in one way or another from soybeans, soy sauces add a depth of complex umami flavor to most all foods and are exceptionally compatible with mushrooms. Many varieties are available outside your average grocery store, online, or in Asian markets. A low-sodium soy sauce is an excellent choice to keep on hand.

- Shoyu, or smoked soy sauce, is unpasteurized and usually organic. It's available in regular smoked and white. It adds a depth of flavor beyond traditional soy sauces.
- Tamari, made from fermented soybeans, has an intense but slightly sweeter flavor than regular soy sauce and contains less sodium— it's a gluten-free alternative to traditional soy sauce.
- Liquid aminos are also made from soybeans but are gluten-free and have a mild, somewhat sweeter flavor with a taste similar to low-sodium soy sauce.

salt, and is also available oak-smoked. Taste and compare the different types. A sprinkle of good salt will add volumes to the flavor of any dish.

Pink-colored Himalayan salt, a popular salt option, is hand harvested from one of the oldest and largest salt mines in the world—the Khewra Salt Mine located in Pakistan, near the Himalayas. This natural processing results in a mineral-enriched salt, free of additives. The small amount of increased minerals contained in the salt are unlikely to provide any significant health benefits. Still, it's a nice salt to have on hand if you prefer a naturally processed salt.

Whichever salt you choose, use it consistently and become familiar with it. All salts aren't created equal, with some tasting saltier and containing more sodium than others. A standard everyday salt is a good kosher salt, Diamond Crystal and Morton are two popular brands.

## SPICES AND SEASONINGS

Find good sources and buy small amounts. You will want to replace your dried herbs and spices every six months. Fennel, oregano, parsley, rosemary, sage, tarragon, and thyme complement mushrooms.

# STOCK CONCENTRATES

There are many excellent-quality stock concentrates and pastes now available. Better Than Bouillon and Minor's are my two favorite brands. As a base for a homemade stock or as a flavor enhancer for soups or sauces, you'll always find them useful in the pantry. Don't be afraid to blend two stocks together (chicken and vegetable for instance) for added depth of flavor.

# VINEGARS

Vinegars are a must-have in any cook's pantry. This indispensable ingredient results from a second bacterial fermentation of alcohol or other raw ingredients containing sugar; for instance, beer, fruits, wine, or rice, producing an acetic acid that lends vinegar its tang.

Balsamic, red wine, rice vinegar, sherry vinegar, and white wine vinegar are all vinegars that especially complement mushrooms.

# WINES

Madeira, Marsala, dry red and white wines, and vermouth are all good choices for pairing with mushrooms. Other great choices are Chinese Shaoxing wine, mirin, and sake.

# WOODS FOR SMOKING

If you like the flavor of smoked foods, the best hardwoods for smoking mushrooms are alder, applewood, maple, pecan, and cherrywood. Buy small chips for stovetop smokers or larger chunks for the grill.

## WINE AND MUSHROOMS

The variety of mushroom you are using in your dish will help guide you to the best wine choice. (Although don't be afraid to bend the rules!)

Oyster, beech, button, and chanterelle mushrooms pair nicely with crisp white wines, while deeper flavored earthy mushrooms like maitake, shiitake, portobellos, porcini, and morels are often better served with reds.

Keep in mind, the sauce and other ingredients you are cooking the mushrooms with play just as much of a role, if not being even more important, in your selection. Rich dishes with creamy or buttery sauces call for white and sparkling wines; game or meat dishes usually pair best with hearty reds.

# HANDY TOOLS

## BLENDER AND FOOD PROCESSOR
For quick chopping or making pâtés, purées, or soups, these are simply a must-have tool for any kitchen. A professional-quality blender or Vitamix is well worth the splurge.

## DEHYDRATOR
If you don't have a convection oven or you will be drying large volumes of mushrooms, this will come in handy for drying your extra mushrooms.

## GLASS JARS
You'll want a few of these for the mushroom conserves and pickles you'll be making. They are also good for storing dried mushrooms, bulk dried herbs, etc.

## GRATER AND MICROPLANE
You'll want more than one for hard cheeses, garlic, and vegetables, and it is a must-have for grating truffles.

## KITCHEN SCALE
Few products are more useful in the kitchen than a digital food scale. They offer precision that rivals the best measuring cups and spoons. Mushrooms vary in weight-to-size ratio and scale. Volume measures, like cups and tablespoons, are notoriously imprecise. A good kitchen scale allows you to be exact about the amount of any ingredient while reducing cleanup time since you can skip the spoons and cups.

## MORTAR AND PESTLE
A kitchen tool straight from the Stone Age! A food processor will make a quick and acceptable pesto, but if you enjoy eating and making authentic pestos, you'll likely want to invest in a stone or wood mortar and pestle. The little extra time and work are worth the improved flavor and texture you'll experience after grinding fresh herbs by hand.

## MUSHROOM BRUSH
You may want a small, slightly stiff brush for cleaning dirt off your mushrooms without using water. One may come in handy before storing foraged mushrooms; they should only be rinsed (if absolutely needed) right before cooking.

Buy a mushroom brush at a specialty store online, or use a short, stiff paintbrush.

## PAPER LUNCH BAGS
These will come in handy for storing your extra mushrooms in the refrigerator.

## SIZZLER PLATES
Very handy, these take the place of large sheet pans. You'll love having these for roasting small amounts of mushrooms.

## SPICE GRINDER
This is an essential tool for turning your dried mushrooms into powders and salts. A spice or coffee grinder can quickly transform your favorite spices, seeds, and herbs into custom blends.

## SPRAY BOTTLE
Use for adding a spritz on rice if the top layer dries out while cooking, on baked goods, or fill with stock for adding moisture to roasts.

# COOKING METHODS

Let's dive right into the most common methods for cooking mushrooms!

## BRAISING

Sear mushrooms in butter and oil over medium-high heat, deglaze the pan with wine, add stock halfway up the mushrooms, turn the heat to medium-low, cover, and simmer gently until tender. Uncover and cook for an additional 3 to 4 minutes to reduce the stock; adjust the seasoning. And for a luxurious sauce, remove from the heat and stir in a small chunk or two of cold butter.

## SAUTÉING

A tried-and-true classic method for preparing mushrooms. In a sauté, the ingredients are quickly cooked with a small amount of fat in a pan large enough to cook the ingredients in one layer, allowing steam to escape and caramelizing to begin.

Heat butter and oil in a large saucepan over medium-high heat. Add the mushrooms in one layer and stir quickly until all the mushrooms are coated with oil. Let the mushrooms cook undisturbed for a few minutes. Once they begin to brown, add salt and stir. Continue to cook, occasionally stirring, until the mushrooms are nicely caramelized. Taste, and adjust the seasoning with salt and black pepper and finish with a splash of wine and a sprinkling of fresh herbs.

## DRY SAUTÉING

A method popular for sautéing mushrooms that contain a high amount of moisture or those wishing to cut down on oil-fat consumption, this method uses little oil. Use fresh mushrooms; older mushrooms or those containing little moisture will not work as well using this method.

Place a medium to large heavy saucepan or skillet (nonstick is fine) over medium-high heat. When the pan is hot, add the mushrooms and salt (work in batches if necessary to avoid crowding the pan). The mushrooms will release and then reabsorb their liquid. When the mushrooms are almost dry, add a tablespoon of butter, ghee, or oil. (If adding garlic, this is the time.) Stir and cook for a minute or two longer until the mushrooms are golden and crispy on the edges. Add a splash of wine and fresh herbs if you like. Toss and remove from the heat to cool. Use in your favorite recipe or indulge straight from the pan.

## ROASTING

A favorite food memory of mine is a special lunch shared with family in Athens, Greece, at

# SUBSTITUTIONS

Mushrooms are usually interchangeable in most recipes. Before giving up on a dish because of a lack of an exotic mushroom, read to find out if the recipe can be made with another variety.

# MUSHROOM CONVERSION CHART

All are estimates. Mushroom varieties vary by weight due to their water content. Here are a few conversions you might find useful:

1 pound fresh = 6 to 7 cups sliced or chopped

8 ounces fresh = 3 to 4 cups sliced or chopped

4 ounces fresh = $1\frac{1}{2}$ to 2 cups sliced or chopped

3 tablespoons whole dried mushrooms = 1 tablespoon powdered mushrooms

1 tablespoon powdered mushrooms = 4 ounces fresh mushrooms

$\frac{1}{4}$ ounce dried mushrooms = scant $\frac{1}{4}$ cup dried mushrooms

$\frac{1}{2}$ ounce dried mushrooms = scant $\frac{1}{2}$ cup dried mushrooms

1 ounce dried mushrooms = scant 1 cup dried mushrooms

# SMOKING SKILLET

You can purchase a stovetop smoker online or make your own. Making a cold-smoking pan for the stovetop is easy, you just need a few items you likely already have:

- A 10-inch stainless-steel saucepan or deep skillet with a tight-fitting lid
- Aluminum foil
- A small (9-inch), round wire rack

Line the skillet with aluminum foil. Spread out 2 to 3 tablespoons of smoker chips evenly on the foil and set the wire rack on top of the foil. Arrange the mushrooms on the rack and place the skillet over medium-high heat. Once the wood begins to smoke, cover with the lid and turn the heat down to medium-low. Smoke for 2 to 5 minutes, depending on the mushroom type and size, and quantity of mushrooms you are smoking. With a large amount, rearrange mushrooms midway to ensure even smoking.

A variety of wood chips is available online. Look for those meant for tabletop smokers.

For smoking larger quantities of mushrooms, use a deeper saucepan or a stockpot with a collapsible strainer.

an outdoor café many years ago. The waiter brought us a beautiful platter of shiitake mushrooms simply roasted in olive oil and garlic, drizzled with aioli and served with wonderful crispy, grilled bread—heavenly!

I think about that dish every time I roast mushrooms. And maybe that's why roasting mushrooms is still my favorite way to prepare them. Roasting concentrates the flavor of the mushrooms more effectively than any other method.

Preheat your oven to 425 degrees F. Toss the mushrooms with a mixture of oil and your seasonings of preference. Roast for 15 to 25 minutes, depending on the size and thickness of the mushrooms. Stir occasionally and add a sprinkle of fresh herbs, smoked salt, or a drizzle of oil before serving.

## GRILLING

Grilled mushrooms are quick, easy, and a versatile stand-alone snack or side dish for steaks or other grilled meats.

Large mushrooms, like full-size oysters or portobello caps, can be placed directly on the grill. Caps are best suited for skewers (soak wooden skewers in water for 20 minutes before grilling), and sliced or smaller mushrooms can be grilled in aluminum foil packets. Coat your mushrooms with oil and season them before placing them on the grill or skewers. For a juicy interior and added flavor, marinate the mushrooms before grilling.

Start over medium direct heat for 2 to 3 minutes, or until grill marks appear, then move to indirect heat to finish cooking for an additional 3 to 4 minutes.

If you're cooking in foil, drizzle the mushrooms with oil and add seasonings before closing the foil packet. Place on indirect, medium to medium-high heat and cook for 20 to 25 minutes, turning halfway through the cooking time.

## STOVETOP SMOKING

The mushrooms need to be dense to hold up well for smoking—think hearty oyster varieties, king trumpet, shiitake, button, cremini, portobello, button, chanterelles, or thickly sliced maitake.

Alder, apple, cherry, and pecan woods are all excellent choices for smoking. Their mild, light smoke tends to enhance, not overpower, the flavor of the mushrooms. Mushrooms absorb smoke flavor quickly and can become sour when smoked with more robust wood flavors like oak, mesquite, or hickory.

As a rule, do not smoke for more than 2 to 3 minutes, or you risk overpowering them with a too-smoky, sour flavor. With a large quantity or large-size mushrooms, you may want to smoke a little longer. Try a taste test on a mushroom after a minute or two.

After smoking, finish on the grill or sauté on the stovetop and add them to your favorite dish.

# PRESERVATION

Now that you've foraged or purchased your mushrooms, you'll want to preserve them as long as possible. Depending on their age, moisture content, and variety, some will last longer than others, and some seem to prefer one storage method over another. One fact is universal; all mushrooms need air to breathe, while at the same time they need to retain moisture. **All mushrooms need to be stored in the refrigerator.**

Once home, make sure to store your mushrooms whole. Only purchase pre-sliced mushrooms if you're planning to use them right away. Mushrooms deteriorate much faster after they are sliced or chopped.

Avoid using water to clean your mushrooms before storing them. Brushing off or wiping to remove excess dirt is fine, but mushrooms will absorb water. If you absolutely must give them a rinse, first pat with a towel and then thoroughly air-dry before storing them.

Save your crisper drawer for vegetables—it's far too humid and has too little airflow for mushrooms. The lowest shelf in your refrigerator is the best place to keep your mushrooms.

Check the mushrooms every other day. Discard any that become wet or slimy. If you've wrapped them in paper towels, change out any that become damp.

## SHORT-TERM STORAGE

### LEAVE THEM IN THEIR COMMERCIAL PACKAGING

You might be surprised to know that mushrooms can thrive in their original packaging. Commercially packaged buttons and cremini will usually hold up well for several days if left unopened. The materials in the cartons are air permeable and the plastic wrap is punctured, providing a perfect mushroom environment. Once opened, re-cover with new plastic wrap and re-puncture with a few holes.

### LOOSELY WRAP IN PAPER TOWELS AND STORE IN A BROWN PAPER BAG

Overall, this method is likely the most successful way to keep the majority of mushrooms. Exceptions are thin, delicate mushrooms that dry out quickly.

The double layer of paper towel and paper insulates and still allows for airflow while absorbing excess moisture.

(Brown bags are preferable to white as they are eco-friendly and produced with fewer chemicals.)

Although this is a popular method and will keep your mushrooms just fine for a couple of days, brown paper is permeable, and the mushrooms may tend to dry out.

# CLEANING MUSHROOMS

It's never fun biting into a gritty mushroom after all the effort you've put into making your delicious dish. Whether foraged or store-bought, be sure to clean the mushrooms well before cooking.

If you've bought or foraged "earthy" mushrooms, don't be tempted to store them in the refrigerator without cleaning them first. The dirt will tend to dry on the mushrooms and become much more difficult to remove later. Most dirt can be removed with a soft brush or damp towel. You may want to purchase a mushroom brush specifically designed for this purpose, although a small, short painter's brush or even a soft toothbrush will do.

For especially dirty mushrooms, rinse or soak them briefly in cold water and lightly scrub them, then move them to a towel to air-dry. Never store them wet. Alternatively, you can pat them dry and enjoy them right away in your favorite recipe.

Inspect mushrooms with crevices like chanterelles, morels, and cauliflower mushrooms for hidden dirt and bugs. And look carefully for tiny worms that may have set up house in your porcini. A careful trim and a quick soak in salted water with a squeeze of lemon will kill any bugs remaining.

### LOOSELY WRAP IN PAPER TOWELS AND STORE INSIDE IN AN UNSEALED PLASTIC STORAGE BAG

This is a preferred method to keep thin, delicate mushrooms like black trumpets, yellow foot chanterelles, yellow oyster mushrooms, and morels. These varieties tend to dry out quickly when stored in paper bags or towels.

Check the paper towels every other day and change them if damp.

### STORE IN PARCHMENT PAPER

This is a good way to store mushrooms, caps in particular. Center the mushrooms on a long sheet of parchment paper, fold the paper over the mushrooms and crimp the edges, creating a closed packet. Place on the bottom shelf of the refrigerator.

This method works better to preserve moisture than storing in paper bags—parchment paper is less porous and helps keep mushrooms from drying out.

### WRAP IN A CLEAN, LINT-FREE KITCHEN TOWEL

Most mushrooms lose too much moisture with this method. The method does work well for larger bracket-type mushrooms and those that require more airflow than moisture retention.

## FREEZING

Freezing allows for longer-term storage, usually for months. Your mushrooms will remain mostly intact and hopefully without a significant loss of flavor or texture.

There are a few mushrooms that survive a direct freeze. These include matsutake, maitake, porcini, chicken of the woods, and lobster mushrooms. For the best results, clean, trim, and, if necessary, cut the mushrooms into pieces or slices, then place them on baking trays in a single layer. Freeze until solid, and store in airtight freezer bags or containers.

Most other mushrooms need to be cooked before freezing due to their high water content and to preserve the best texture after thawing. Sauté them in butter or oil, let cool, freeze on trays, and then store them in airtight containers for up to six months. If you have leftover cooked mushrooms in a sauce, freeze them directly in an airtight container or freezer bag, removing as much air as possible.

## DRYING, POWDERS, AND SALTS

### DRYING

Drying is likely the most efficient method for preserving mushrooms long term. Once dried, you can easily add the flavor of your favorite

mushrooms to an endless variety of dishes. Dried mushrooms (with only a few exceptions), will *not* hydrate to the volume of their fresh counterparts. Your dishes, however, will benefit from the intense flavor dried mushrooms offer. Virtually any mushroom can be dried, though some are more suited than others. Porcini, shiitake, and morels are a few of the best choices for drying and making stocks or powders. Dried reishi, lion's mane, and cordyceps have tremendous health benefits, surpassing their gourmet qualities, and are ideal for making teas and tinctures.

This drying method works with all mushroom varieties, though the process will be quicker with thin, smaller mushrooms like beech or smaller trumpets. First, clean the mushrooms of all dirt and debris, then cut them into equal-size pieces no larger than $1/2$ inch thick. Dry in a dehydrator according to directions or scatter on a baking sheet and place in a convection oven for about 6 to 10 hours at 100 degrees F, or a regular oven at 110 to 125 degrees F. Leave the door slightly open to allow moisture to escape. Turn the pieces occasionally and leave in the oven until the mushrooms are completely dry and crispy.

Once cooled, the mushrooms can be stored in an airtight container at room temperature or in the refrigerator or freezer for optimum freshness. Properly dried and stored mushrooms will keep for a year or more.

If you often have a surplus of mushrooms, you may want to invest in a dehydrator. For most of us, though, a conventional (ideally convection) oven works fine. During summer months, you can dry your mushrooms outside in the sun, providing an extra dose of vitamin D.

Rehydrate dried mushrooms by soaking them in hot or simmering water, stock, or wine for about 20 minutes. Drain and pat dry, chop, and sauté before adding to your mushroom dishes and soups or gravies. The strained soaking liquid will give a glorious burst of mushroom essence to sauces and stews.

## POWDERS

Dried mushrooms can be ground into a powder using a spice grinder. Mix with other seasonings, chili powders, or dried herbs to create a mushroom rub for coating steaks or roasts.

One tablespoon of powder equals 4 ounces of fresh mushrooms as a replacement when used to flavor dishes.

## SALTS

A sprinkle of mushroom salt adds a burst of umami flavor to vegetables, chicken, and even eggs. Use when cooking "ordinary" mushrooms to boost the mushroom flavor.

To make mushroom salt, combine 1 cup of sea salt with every $1/4$ cup of ground mushrooms. Adding a little chili, garlic, or onion powder will punch up the flavor even more. Store in an airtight container.

# PICKLING AND CONSERVAS

I never met a pickled mushroom I didn't like! Gather up your extra mushrooms, a variety is good. It's always nice to have a jar on hand even if you can't resist snacking on them. A good vinegary marinade and a quick boil will ensure tangy, tasty mushrooms that will keep for a month or more. Pickling uses vinegar and spices, while conservas are mostly oil-based.

Try the Pickled Pioppini (page 193) or the Wild Mushroom Conserva (page 100) to get you started.

# BLACK TRUMPET SALT

Makes about 1 1/4 cups

3/4 cup dried black trumpet
   mushrooms
3/4 cup sea salt
1/4 cup Maldon oak-smoked salt

Enjoy this smoky, flavorful mushroom finishing salt on grilled chicken, fish, or vegetables. Replace the trumpets with morels or porcini, or try lobster mushrooms for a seafood seasoning or finishing salt.

Place the dried trumpets into a spice grinder and blend until smooth. Remove to a bowl. Add the salts to the grinder and blend to your preference, from coarse to fine grind. Thoroughly stir the salts and mushroom powder together and store in an airtight container for up to 6 months.

# FORAGED VERSUS CULTIVATED

Decisions, decisions!

Which are the healthiest? The tastiest?

Like most things in life, there are pros and cons to both types of mushrooms.

Wide varieties of commercially cultivated mushrooms are available in your local markets, grocery stores, and even online. You can eat them without worry, and the quality is generally very good. And cultivated mushrooms have all the health benefits of foraged mushrooms. You can even grow your own. Cultivating at home is easy and fun!

If you're ambitious, there's an excitement to watching mushrooms grow from a substrate you've carefully prepared and seeded with the cultures of a favorite mushroom and evolve into magnificent, tasty mushrooms. Sometimes the process can be frustrating, but the result is almost always worthwhile.

An easy alternative for home-growing, ready-to-go mushroom blocks are available from mushroom growers or online. Several varieties are usually available, and with each block, you might enjoy two or three harvests simply from placing a box under a light on your kitchen counter.

As for taste, foraged mushrooms tend to have a more intense flavor than cultivated mushrooms, even of the same species. Cultivated mushrooms may be milder but they also have consistency in taste since they're grown on a sterilized compost mixture or substrate. And with foraged, of course, there's the added thrill of the "hunt." The discovery of a patch of a sought-after favorite (like morels in spring) or a surprise find of delectable and elusive mushrooms can be a gratifying experience. And whether cut or plucked, the mycelium continues to grow underground, so you likely will find another patch of them growing in the same place the following season.

Some of the most flavorful wild mushrooms are mycorrhizal—those sharing a root system through their mycelium with other plants and trees. These are prized, desirable mushrooms that are almost impossible to cultivate. Morels, chanterelles, and porcini are good examples.

If you're new to foraging, the best idea, of course, is to go with an experienced guide. You might find a local mushroom foraging group in your area that offers guided hunting tours. If you're going it alone, invest in a couple of good foraging handbooks and start with the near foolproof, uniquely identifiable "safe" species with non-poisonous look-alikes: varieties like lion's mane, black trumpets, and oysters.

Be careful when eating any foraged mushroom. If in doubt, contact an experienced forager. And once you've determined it's safe, limit the number of mushrooms you eat of a variety you have not had before. Some mushrooms can cause gastrointestinal issues. So as tempting as it may be to sauté a large plate of delicious, foraged mushrooms, try a sampling first!

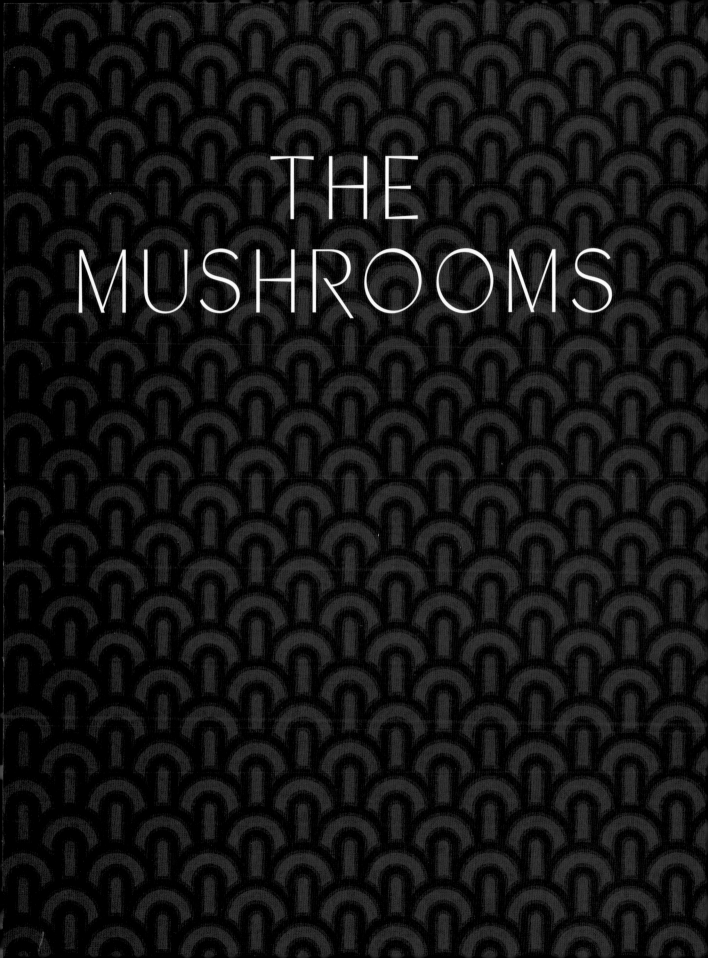

# THE MUSHROOMS

BEECH (SHIMEJI) *Hypsizygus tessulatus*

# BEECH MUSHROOMS

BEECH MUSHROOMS grow in clusters with marble-size round caps perched on thin, elegant stems. These petite mushrooms are popular with chefs and enthusiastic cooks, not only for their unique, whimsical appearance, but also for their intense flavor, crunchy texture, and suitability for a wide range of preparations.

Though difficult to cultivate, a few countries, primarily China, have grown them successfully, making them readily available worldwide.

There are two varieties of these unique mushrooms: brown and white. The brown are known as Buna-shimeji, Japanese honey mushroom, or brown beech, and they have an umami (savory) flavor. The white variety is known as Bunapi-shimeji, or white beech. They have a flavor reminiscent of seafood, which is why they are often referred to as Alba Clamshell or seafood mushrooms.

## NUTRITIONAL VALUE

These little mushrooms pack in a fair amount of nutrients. High in selenium, beta-glucans (aids in regulating blood sugar), and B vitamins, including thiamine, riboflavin, and niacin, they also contain high levels of copper and potassium.

## SELECTION AND STORAGE

Look for fresh dry-looking mushrooms with few brown spots. You may find them packaged in plastic, a method that works fine for temporary storage. Once opened, tuck them into parchment paper or wrap them in paper towels, place the bundle in a paper bag, and store in the refrigerator.

## COOKING METHODS

Braise, deep-fry, pickle, roast, smoke, steam, stir-fry

## CULINARY USES

Uncooked shimeji are of little nutritional value. These mushrooms are safe to eat raw in salads, but you'll want to pair them with a dressing that will stand up to their pungent and slightly bitter taste. Cooking brings out their nutty, buttery flavor and the texture remains crisp. Sauté and serve them alongside or over a meat or fish course, add them to soups and stir-fries, or fry them in tempura.

## FLAVOR PAIRINGS

- Bell pepper, red
- Butter
- Chicken
- Cilantro
- Citrus
- Eggs
- Fish: cod, salmon
- Garlic
- Green beans
- Herbs, fresh: basil, cilantro, parsley, tarragon
- Hoisin
- Lemon
- Miso
- Noodles: soba, udon, vermicelli
- Olive oil
- Onion
- Peas
- Poultry
- Rabbit
- Rice
- Scallions
- Sesame, oil and seeds
- Soy, tamari, shoyu
- Wine, white

# CREAMY BEECH MUSHROOM AND SUN-DRIED TOMATO BUCATINI

Serves 2

Vegetarian

8 ounces bucatini, thick spaghetti, or another long pasta
2 tablespoons olive oil or butter
1 garlic clove, thinly sliced
1 large shallot, halved and thinly
  sliced
5 ounces Buna-shimeji
  (brown beech) mushrooms,
  trimmed and cleaned, larger
  ones halved lengthwise
  (about 2$\frac{1}{2}$ cups)
$\frac{1}{2}$ teaspoon kosher salt, plus
  more as needed
2 tablespoons dry white wine
$\frac{1}{3}$ cup thinly sliced oil-packed
  sun-dried tomatoes
$\frac{1}{3}$ cup Quick Mushroom Broth
  (page 230) or vegetable
  stock
$\frac{1}{3}$ cup heavy cream
Freshly ground black pepper
$\frac{1}{4}$ cup grated Parmesan cheese,
  plus more for serving
Small handful torn fresh basil
  leaves

This is an easy dish made with sun-dried tomatoes, basil, white wine, and beech mushrooms, tossed with Parmesan cheese over long pasta. Simple and delicious. This recipe doubles nicely if you need to serve more than two.

Bring a large pot of lightly salted water to a boil over high heat. Add the bucatini and cook for 8 to 10 minutes, or until al dente. Reserve 1 cup of the pasta water. Drain the rest and set the pasta aside.

Heat the oil in a large, deep skillet over medium-low heat and sauté the garlic and shallot for 3 to 4 minutes until just softened. Raise the heat to medium, stir in the mushrooms, sprinkle with the salt, and cook for 5 to 6 minutes, or until lightly golden.

Add the wine and cook for about 1 minute until it's absorbed. Stir in the tomatoes, stock, and heavy cream and cook for 5 to 6 minutes at a low simmer. Taste, and adjust the seasoning with salt and a few good twists of freshly ground black pepper.

Add the pasta to the sauce and toss thoroughly. Stir in some of the reserved pasta water, a little at a time, to smooth and tighten the sauce. Stir in the cheese and basil leaves and toss again to coat the pasta. Serve topped with additional grated Parmesan.

# BEECH MUSHROOM AND
# GREEN BEAN CASSEROLE

1 pound fresh green beans, trimmed

2 tablespoons olive oil or butter, plus more as needed

2 shallots, thinly sliced lengthwise

4 slices (about 1 ounce) Serrano ham halved crosswise and cut into ½-inch strips

1 teaspoon honey

4 ounces Buna-shimeji (brown beech) mushrooms, trimmed and cleaned, larger ones halved lengthwise (about 2 cups)

2 tablespoons Amontillado or other medium-dry sherry

½ cup heavy cream

½ cup Roasted Mushroom Stock (page 232), vegetable stock, or chicken stock

Kosher salt

Freshly ground black pepper

Toasted and chopped Marcona almonds, for garnish

A Spanish take on the traditional green bean casserole, this version includes Serrano ham, Marcona almonds, and a touch of sherry. It's a little lighter than the original, but still creamy and delicious.

Brown beech mushrooms with their almost sweet, nutty flavor are a perfect fit for this dish.

Preheat the oven to 350 degrees F.

Fill a large bowl of water with ice.

Bring a large pot of salted water to a boil over high heat. Add the beans and blanch them for 2 to 3 minutes. Drain and place the green beans in the ice water to stop the cooking.

In a large skillet, warm the oil over medium-low heat. Add the shallots and sauté for 2 to 3 minutes, or until softened. Increase the heat to medium-high, add the Serrano ham and honey, and quickly sauté for 1 to 2 minutes, or until the ham begins to caramelize. Add the mushrooms, adding more oil if necessary, and sauté for 4 to 5 minutes, or until the mushrooms are cooked through and golden.

Stir in the sherry and cook until it is absorbed. Stir in the cream and stock and remove from the heat. Drain the green beans, add them to the skillet, and toss everything together thoroughly. Taste, and adjust the seasoning with salt and lots of pepper, as needed. Transfer into a casserole dish, sprinkle the Marcona almonds over the top, and bake for 20 to 25 minutes, or until the almonds are lightly browned and the mixture is nice and bubbly. Let the casserole rest for 10 to 15 minutes before serving.

# POLYNESIAN PORK MEI FUN WITH BUNA-SHIMEJI

**MARINADE**

1 tablespoon honey

1 1/2 teaspoons fresh lime juice

1 teaspoon low-sodium soy
   sauce

1 teaspoon chili powder

1/4 teaspoon ground cumin

1/2 teaspoon kosher salt

6 ounces pork tenderloin,
   halved lengthwise and cut
   into thin 1/2 × 2-inch slices

Mei Fun is one of my favorite dishes, in all of its many variations. Silky vermicelli noodles tossed in a light, flavorful sauce mixed with bits of meat and crispy vegetables is a combination I can rarely resist.

This Polynesian version includes tender, lean pork tenderloin, chiles, pineapple, bok choy, and brown beech mushrooms tossed with noodles in a gingery, pineapple-sesame sauce. Macadamia nuts add a crunchy finishing touch.

Substitute a wider rice noodle, or angel hair pasta if you prefer. You may also exchange the pork for chicken, shrimp, or tofu.

---

**TO MAKE THE MARINADE,** combine the honey, lime juice, soy sauce, chili powder, cumin, and salt in a medium bowl. Add the pork tenderloin and mix until thoroughly coated. Cover and place in the refrigerator to marinate for at least 3 hours or up to overnight.

*continued »*

## MEI FUN

6 ounces vermicelli rice noodles

2 tablespoons grapeseed oil, divided, plus more as needed

4 ounces Buna-shimeji (brown beech) mushrooms, trimmed and larger ones halved lengthwise (about 2 cups)

1 garlic clove, minced

1 to 2 fresh chiles, thinly sliced (depending on how spicy you like your Mei Fun)

1/2 teaspoon minced peeled fresh ginger

1/3 cup pineapple juice

2 teaspoons low-sodium soy sauce

1/2 teaspoon sesame oil

2 tablespoons coconut oil

1/2 medium sweet onion, cut into 1/4-inch slices lengthwise

1/2 red bell pepper, diced

Pinch of kosher salt

1/2 cup diced pineapple

2 cups chopped bok choy

2 green onions, green parts only, chopped

1/2 cup toasted, salted macadamia nuts, finely chopped

Fresh lime wedges, for serving

**TO MAKE THE MEI FUN,** bring a large pot of water to a boil over high heat and boil the vermicelli for 1 to 2 minutes (the noodles will be slightly underdone). Rinse with cold water and drain. Using kitchen shears, cut the noodles into 5- to 6-inch-long pieces.

Remove the pork from the marinade and pat dry.

Heat a large skillet over medium-high heat, add 1 tablespoon of grapeseed oil, and sear the pork on all sides. Lower the heat to medium and cook for 3 to 4 minutes for medium-well, or until done to your preference. Transfer the pork to a plate and let rest.

Add the shimeji to the pan and cook, adding more oil if necessary, for 5 to 6 minutes, or until golden and cooked through. Transfer the mushrooms to the plate with the cooked pork.

Wipe out the skillet, place it over medium heat, add the remaining 1 tablespoon of grapeseed oil, and sauté the garlic for 1 to 2 minutes, or until tender. Add the chiles, ginger, pineapple juice, soy sauce, and sesame oil. Cook for 2 to 3 minutes, or until slightly syrupy. Remove from the heat and pour the pineapple sauce into a small bowl.

Raise the heat to medium-high, add the coconut oil to the skillet, and sauté the onion and bell pepper with a pinch of salt for 2 to 3 minutes. Add the pineapple and bok choy and sauté for an additional minute. Add the pork, mushrooms, and noodles to the skillet and toss until well mixed. Add the pineapple sauce and green onions and continue to toss and cook for 1 to 2 minutes, or until heated through.

Serve topped with the chopped macadamias nuts and lime wedges for a squeeze of juice.

# SHIMEJI AND
# SWEET CHILE SLAW

Makes 2 cups

Vegetarian with vegan option

3 tablespoons rice vinegar

1 1/2 tablespoons sesame oil

2 teaspoons fresh lemon juice

1 tablespoon honey or agave
syrup

1 garlic clove, grated

1 teaspoon grated peeled fresh
ginger

1 tablespoon grapeseed oil or
other neutral oil

1 1/2 ounces Bunapi-shimeji
(white beech) mushrooms,
ends trimmed (about 2/3 cup)

3 ounces cucumber, julienned
(about 1/2 cup)

3 ounces red chile pepper,
julienned (about 1/2 cup)

3 ounces yellow bell pepper,
julienned (about 1/2 cup)

3 green onions, green parts
only, thinly sliced

Kosher salt

Freshly ground black pepper

This quick, tangy slaw is perfect for topping cold Asian noodles
or burgers. For a chopped slaw variation, transfer the vegetables to a food processor and pulse until chopped to preference
before mixing with the dressing.

Whisk together the vinegar, sesame oil, lemon juice, honey, garlic and
ginger in a medium bowl.

In a medium skillet, heat the grapeseed oil over medium-high heat.
Add the mushrooms and sauté for 2 to 3 minutes, or until just
cooked through.

Transfer the mushrooms to the bowl with the vinegar mixture. Add the
cucumber, chile pepper, bell pepper, and green onions and toss until
well coated with the dressing. Place the bowl in the refrigerator to chill.
Taste, and season with salt and pepper just before serving.

# BLACK TRUMPET
### *Craterellus cornucopioides*

BLACK TRUMPET mushrooms, also known as the Horn of Plenty, will likely be one of the tastiest mushrooms you'll eat. A cousin to chanterelles, you'll find them growing in late summer in eastern North America. On the West Coast, they grow from winter to early spring. Dusty brownish black in color, hollow, and vessel shaped, they emerge strikingly from the ground in mossy, damp areas under primarily broad-leaved beech or oak trees. They blend into the forest floor, so look carefully, they are easy to miss. As frustrating as they may be to forage, I assure you, you'll find them well worth the effort. While they are in season, they are usually available to purchase fresh online as well as dried.

## NUTRITIONAL VALUE

The black trumpet contains a considerable amount of vitamin B12, more so than most other mushrooms. This essential vitamin plays a vital role in the formation of red blood cells, as well as in cell metabolism and nerve function.

## SELECTION AND STORAGE

Inspect trumpets for discolored or soft spots. Fresh specimens should be elastic and firm with an appealing, almost apricot aroma.

Black trumpets are delicate and love moisture. If you find or source them fresh, wrap them in paper towels and tuck them into a plastic freezer or storage bag. Leave the bag unsealed and store it on the lower shelf of the refrigerator. Check and replace the paper towels every other day if they become damp. Discard trumpets that become slimy or wet-black in color. And they should smell fresh and fruity. Throw out any or all that are beginning to smell "off."

To freeze black trumpets, first give them a quick blanch in boiling water. Cool and then freeze them in a single layer on a baking sheet. Once frozen, pack them into freezer-safe containers. You can also sauté the mushrooms in butter or oil before freezing. Frozen black trumpets will keep for one or two months in the freezer.

Likely the best way to preserve trumpets long term is to dry them (see page 24). Drying intensifies their deep, woodsy flavor. Ground into a powder, they add depth to stews and sauces and make delicious salts and butters.

## COOKING METHODS

Bake, fry, sauté, stir-fry

## COOKING TIPS

These "poor man's truffles" are at the top of my list of favorite mushrooms. Trumpets are full of deep, smoky mushroom flavor and cook to a velvety texture. They are wonderful simply pan-seared in butter and tossed with fresh herbs, and they also make fantastic pasta dishes and risottos. Black trumpets pair beautifully with eggs, chicken, or fish and it's best to cook them in dishes that allow them to shine rather than overpowering them with strong flavors.

Dried trumpets make a delicious, smoky stock that gives deep rich flavor to most any sauce recipe for use with red meats or pork.

## FLAVOR PAIRINGS

- Butter
- Citrus
- Cheese: cream, goat, ricotta
- Eggs
- Fish: cod, salmon, white fish
- Garlic
- Ham
- Herbs, fresh: basil, parsley, tarragon
- Lemon
- Olive oil
- Pasta
- Pork
- Potatoes
- Poultry
- Rice
- Shallots
- Squash
- Wine, white

# EGGS COCOTTE WITH BLACK TRUMPETS

Serves 4

Vegetarian

2 tablespoons butter, divided, plus more for the ramekins

1 large leek, white part only, halved, cleaned, and thinly sliced

$\frac{2}{3}$ cup finely chopped black trumpet mushrooms

2 teaspoons dry sherry

6 tablespoons heavy cream, divided

Kosher salt

Freshly ground black pepper

4 large eggs

$\frac{1}{4}$ cup grated Gruyère cheese

2 tablespoons minced fresh chives or parsley

Buttered toast or grilled bread, for dipping

This is a classic French egg dish, and if you like a soft egg yolk and a drizzle of cream with crispy toast, you're going to love this recipe. And once you master the technique of baking the eggs just right, you'll likely be making it often. Try using other vegetables, swapping out the cheese, and getting a little creative. Once it's in the oven, watch it carefully; the eggs cook quickly. Depending on your oven and the size of the ramekins, your timing for perfect doneness will vary. This would be made even more decadent with a fresh-shaved truffle.

Preheat the oven to 350 degrees F.

In a medium skillet over medium heat, melt 1 tablespoon of the butter. Add the leek and sauté for 4 to 5 minutes, or until softened; transfer to a plate.

Add the remaining 1 tablespoon of butter to the pan, add the chopped black trumpets, and sauté for 6 to 8 minutes, or until the mushrooms have released and reabsorbed their liquid. Stir in the sherry and cook briefly until absorbed. Add 2 tablespoons of the heavy cream, give it a quick stir, and remove the pan from the heat. Add the leek back to the pan and mix well. Season with salt and pepper.

Lightly grease four ramekins with butter. Divide the leek and mushroom mixture among the ramekins and, using a spoon, make an indent in the mixture to hold the eggs. Crack an egg into a small bowl and slide it into a ramekin. Then drizzle with 1 tablespoon of cream and sprinkle with 1 tablespoon of cheese. Repeat for the remaining three ramekins.

Bring a small pot of water to a boil over high heat.

Place the ramekins in a baking dish and carefully pour enough boiling water in the baking dish to reach about three-fourths of the way up the sides of the ramekins.

Transfer the baking dish to the oven and bake for 13 to 15 minutes, or until the egg whites are set and the yolks are still soft. Carefully remove the baking dish from the oven (be careful not to splash water into the ramekins) and, using tongs, transfer the ramekins to plates. Garnish each with chives (and maybe a shaving of truffle) and serve with lightly buttered toast alongside, and swoon!

# CHANTILLY POTATOES WITH TRUFFLED BLACK TRUMPETS

2 tablespoons butter, plus more for the casserole dish

2 ounces black trumpet mushrooms (fresh or dehydrated), chopped into $1/2$-inch pieces (about 1 cup)

$1/2$ teaspoon Truffle Salt (See Salts, page 25) or regular salt

Kosher salt

3 pounds Yukon gold potatoes, peeled and cut into $1^1/2$-inch cubes

$1^1/2$ cups cold heavy cream

$1^1/2$ cups grated Gruyère cheese or a mixture of Parmesan and Gruyère

Chantilly potatoes are a pure indulgence. Heavy cream is whipped to stiff peaks, folded into smooth potatoes, topped with more whipped cream and Gruyère cheese, and broiled until golden. Black trumpets and a hint of truffle salt add a depth of umami flavor and further elevate the dish. This is a perfect accompaniment to prime rib or baked ham for the holidays.

A ricer will give a much smoother texture than hand mashing the potatoes, but both will result in a successful dish.

Grease a 2-quart casserole dish with butter and set aside.

Heat the butter in a medium skillet over medium-high heat. Add the mushrooms and sauté for 5 to 6 minutes, or until their liquid has been released and reabsorbed and the mushrooms are just beginning to crisp. Sprinkle with the truffle salt, stir, and set aside.

Bring a large pot of lightly salted water to a boil over high heat. Add the potatoes and cook until a knife can be inserted easily. Drain thoroughly and pass the potatoes through a ricer. Lightly season with salt, mix well, and set aside.

Pour the cold cream into the bowl of a stand mixer fitted with the whisk attachment. Whisk until the cream just forms stiff peaks, about 8 minutes. (You can also use an electric hand mixer or a hand whisk.) Stir a spoonful of the whipped cream into the potatoes until blended, then gently fold in about two-thirds of the whipped cream. Gently spread the potato mixture into the buttered casserole dish.

Preheat the broiler.

Fold 1 cup of the grated cheese into the remaining portion of whipped cream and spread it evenly on top of the potatoes. Sprinkle the remaining cheese over the top. (At this point the casserole can be refrigerated up to overnight. Bring it to room temperature before proceeding.)

Broil for 5 to 6 minutes, or until the top is golden brown. Serve hot.

# ROSSEJAT DE FIDEOS WITH SHRIMP AND BLACK TRUMPETS

## QUICK LEMON-GARLIC AIOLI

1 tablespoon fresh lemon juice,
   plus more as needed

Pinch of crumbled saffron
   threads

2 or 3 peeled garlic cloves

$1/2$ teaspoon kosher salt, plus
   more as needed

1 egg yolk

$1/2$ cup mayonnaise

$1/4$ cup good quality olive oil

Pinch of cayenne pepper

Freshly ground black pepper

Rossejat de Fideos is a traditional seafood dish originating in the Catalonia region of Spain. Resembling paella, the recipe calls for fine, vermicelli-like pasta, or fideos, instead of rice. In this recipe, the pasta is first toasted in olive oil, then cooked slowly in a rich stock made from black trumpets, adding another layer of smoky flavor to this variation of the popular dish.

If you can't find fideos, use Italian dry vermicelli or angel hair pasta broken into 2-inch pieces.

**TO MAKE THE AIOLI,** combine the lemon juice and saffron in a small bowl and let steep for 15 minutes. Using a mortar and pestle or the flat side of a chef's knife, mash the garlic and salt together into a smooth paste. Add to a small bowl with the egg yolk, mayonnaise, lemon juice–saffron mixture, olive oil, and cayenne and whisk to combine. Add salt and black pepper to taste and a squeeze of additional lemon if needed. Cover and set aside. Store covered in the refrigerator for up to 3 days.

## ROSSEJAT DE FIDEOS

1 ounce dried black trumpet
mushrooms, broken into
1-inch pieces (about 1 cup)

2 cups chicken, seafood, or
vegetable stock

3 cups water

1 teaspoon kosher salt, plus
more as needed

3 tablespoons olive oil, divided,
plus more as needed

7 ounces fideos or vermicelli
pasta broken into 2-inch
pieces

$^1/_2$ pound (20 to 21 count)
shrimp, peeled and deveined

Freshly ground black pepper

$^1/_2$ small onion, finely chopped

3 garlic cloves, thinly sliced

1$^1/_2$ teaspoons smoked Spanish
paprika

1 tablespoon double-
concentrated tomato paste

2 tablespoons brandy

Chopped fresh parsley, for
garnish

**TO MAKE THE ROSSEJAT DE FIDEOS,** in a medium saucepan over medium-high heat, combine the dried mushrooms, stock, water, and salt. Bring to a simmer, cover, and cook for 10 minutes, then remove from the heat and set aside to soften.

In a paella pan or a large, deep skillet over medium heat, heat 1 tablespoon of olive oil. Add the fideos and toast them, stirring often, for 10 to 12 minutes, or until golden brown. Transfer the fideos to a bowl and set aside. Add another tablespoon of olive oil to the pan and briefly sear the shrimp until cooked through, about 2 minutes. Season with salt and pepper, then transfer to a small bowl.

Strain the mushrooms from the broth, reserving the broth. Add the mushrooms to the pan and sauté, stirring often, adding more oil if necessary, for 4 to 5 minutes, until slightly crispy. Remove from the pan.

Add the remaining 1 tablespoon of olive oil to the pan and sauté the onion and garlic for 3 to 4 minutes, or until softened. Add the smoked paprika, tomato paste, and brandy and cook, stirring, for 1 to 2 minutes. Stir in 3 cups of the reserved stock-water mixture and simmer for 10 to 15 minutes, or until reduced by about one-third. Taste and adjust the seasoning with salt and pepper.

Stir in the fideos and cooked mushrooms, cover, and cook for 3 minutes. Remove the lid, add 1 cup of the remaining stock-water mixture, and cook, stirring occasionally, for 3 to 5 minutes, or until the noodles are tender and the broth has been absorbed. Add more of the remaining stock-water mixture if necessary. Taste, and adjust the seasoning with salt and pepper.

Preheat the broiler.

**TO SERVE,** arrange the shrimp on top of the fideos and broil for 3 to 5 minutes, or until the noodles are browned and crispy. Drizzle with the aioli and garnish with chopped parsley.

# SPANISH OMELET WITH BLACK TRUMPETS AND CHORIZO

Serves 4 to 6

2 tablespoons, divided, plus
   1 cup olive oil

1½ links (about 4½ ounces)
   chorizo sausage, cut into
   ¼-inch dice

½ cup finely chopped onion

4 ounces fresh or rehydrated
   black trumpet mushrooms,
   cut into ½- to ¾-inch pieces
   (2 cups)

4 or 5 medium Yukon gold or
   russet potatoes, peeled and
   cut into ¼-inch slices (about
   4 cups)

4 eggs

1 teaspoon kosher salt

1 cup grated Manchego cheese,
   divided

Finely chopped green onions
   (green parts only) or fresh
   parsley, for garnish

A classic Spanish appetizer! And one that can be made ahead and served at room temperature.

Serve with Pickled Onions (page 110) or Quick Lemon-Garlic Aioli (page 44).

---

In a large (10-inch) deep, nonstick skillet over medium heat, warm 1 tablespoon of the olive oil. Add the chorizo and sauté for 8 to 10 minutes, or until cooked through. Add the onion and cook, stirring often, for about 5 minutes, or until softened. Add the remaining 1 tablespoon of olive oil, stir in the black trumpets, and cook for 4 to 5 minutes, or until the mushrooms have reabsorbed any liquid. Transfer the mixture to a plate.

Using the same skillet, raise the heat to medium-high and add 1 cup of olive oil. When the oil is hot, carefully add the potatoes, and turn the heat down to medium-low. Cook, turning the potatoes occasionally, for 15 to 20 minutes, or until they are just cooked through. Strain the potatoes, reserving the oil, and transfer the potatoes to a bowl.

Whisk together the eggs and salt in a large bowl. Stir in the cooked onion, chorizo, mushrooms, and half of the cheese. Slowly fold in the potatoes and gently mix.

Add 2 tablespoons of the reserved oil back into the skillet and place it over medium-high heat. When the oil is hot, pour the potato mixture into the pan. Turn the heat to medium-low, and cook, lightly pressing down on the potatoes, for about 5 minutes, or until the eggs are beginning to set and the edges are cooked through.

Carefully flip the skillet, sliding the omelet upside down onto a plate. Slide the omelet back into the pan to finish cooking the other side. Cook for another 4 to 5 minutes, or until lightly browned. Slide the omelet onto a serving plate, sprinkle with the remaining cheese and green onions, cut into slices, and serve.

# CACIO E PEPE WITH ZEBRA LINGUINE AND BLACK TRUMPETS

2 tablespoons butter, divided

4 ounces guanciale or bacon, cut into small dice

4 ounces (2 cups) black trumpet mushrooms (rehydrated or fresh), chopped

8 ounces zebra linguine, regular linguine, or thick spaghetti

¼ cup finely grated Pecorino Romano cheese, at room temperature, plus more for serving

2 tablespoons finely grated Parmesan cheese, plus more for serving

½ teaspoon freshly ground black pepper, plus more as needed

Kosher salt

Cacio e Pepe is simple and easy, and satisfying for breakfast or a late-night quick dinner. Add a soft-fried egg if you like. Rehydrated trumpets amp up the flavors in this vibrant-looking and -tasting dish. Black and white zebra pasta is eye catching, but if you can only find regular linguine, no worries, it's all about the freshly ground pepper!

In a medium saucepan over medium heat, melt 1 tablespoon of butter. Sauté the guanciale, stirring often, until crispy, 6 to 8 minutes, and transfer to a bowl. Add the remaining 1 tablespoon of butter to the pan and sauté the trumpets until they are softened and just beginning to crisp. Transfer to the bowl with the guanciale.

In a large pot over high heat, bring lightly salted water to a boil. Add the pasta and cook for 8 to 10 minutes, or until al dente. Reserve 1 cup of the water, drain the pasta, and set aside.

Add the cheeses and pepper to the saucepan over medium heat and slowly add the reserved pasta water, whisking the cheeses into a creamy sauce. (If you want to add an egg, now is the time to fry it.) Add the pasta to the saucepan with the guanciale and trumpets and toss until warm and well coated with the sauce. Taste and season with salt and additional pepper. If you're adding an egg, place it on top. Serve with extra grated cheese and your favorite pepper mill.

# BUTTON, CREMINI, AND PORTOBELLO

*Agaricus bisporus*

**THIS GROUP** of popular mushrooms accounts for almost 90 percent of the cultivated mushrooms in the U.S. They'll be the ones you are most likely to find in your local supermarket. All are of the same variety, just in different stages of growth. The white button mushrooms are the youngest, the light brown cremini (also called baby bellas) are more mature, and portobellos—the larger and darker brown variety—are the oldest. Mushrooms lose moisture as they age, giving portobellos the flavor advantage, followed by cremini and white buttons.

## NUTRITIONAL VALUE

The Agaricus genus of mushroom is famously nutritious, rich in carbohydrates, proteins, lipids, fibers, and minerals. They have antimicrobial and antioxidant qualities and are believed to help fight cancer, diabetes, and hypertension.

## SELECTION AND STORAGE

Since you will likely be acquiring these mushrooms at your local grocer, look for the freshest looking and most recently packaged containers, and avoid buying any that are pre-sliced unless you are planning to use them right away.

An ideal method for storing unopened cremini and button mushrooms is to leave them in their original packaging. Once opened, replace the plastic wrap and puncture it with a few holes. They also store very well wrapped in paper towels and placed in paper bags.

## COOKING METHODS

Braise, broil, marinate, roast, sauté, stuff

## CULINARY TIPS

Portobellos are an excellent meat substitute due to their hearty texture and flavor. They absorb marinades well and hold up admirably on the grill. Sauté, stew, or roast them, and if you enjoy stuffed mushrooms, they hold a fair amount of filling—enough to be served as a main course. Their smaller cousins can also be stuffed or sautéed, and they are easily incorporated into most any dish.

## FLAVOR PAIRINGS

- Arugula
- Bacon
- Basil
- Bread or breadcrumbs
- Butter
- Cheese: most all cheeses—aged cheddar, goat,

  Parmesan, ricotta, etc.
- Chives
- Crab
- Cream
- Crème fraîche
- Eggs
- Garlic
- Green beans

- Lemon
- Olive oil
- Onions
- Parsley
- Pasta
- Peas
- Pepper
- Polenta
- Shallots

- Soy
- Spinach
- Thyme
- Tomatoes: fresh and sun-dried
- Vinegar: balsamic, sherry
- Wine: Marsala, red, sherry, white

# MUSHROOM AND SPINACH MARIA

1 (6-ounce) package fresh baby spinach, washed, excess water removed, and chopped

4 tablespoons butter, divided

8 ounces cremini mushrooms, trimmed and sliced (about 3$\frac{1}{2}$ cups)

$\frac{1}{2}$ teaspoon kosher salt, plus more as needed

$\frac{1}{4}$ cup finely chopped onion

2 garlic cloves, minced

2 tablespoons all-purpose flour

1 cup milk, warmed

1$\frac{1}{2}$ cups grated Comté, Gruyère, Monterey Jack, or fontina cheese

$\frac{1}{4}$ teaspoon dry mustard

Pinch of ground nutmeg

Pinch of cayenne pepper

Freshly ground black pepper

This recipe is a twist on Spinach Maria, a classic dish originating from Calhoun's, a very popular east Tennessee BBQ joint. Served as a side dish in the restaurant, it's been converted here into an indulgent dip. Usually made with Monterey Jack cheese, in this version, nutty Comté takes its place, and cremini mushrooms add yet another layer of flavor. Serve with crackers or toasted bread.

Preheat the oven to 350 degrees F.

Place the spinach in a large, deep saucepan over medium-high heat. Cook, stirring often, until the spinach is wilted, about 2 minutes. Transfer to a bowl and set aside.

Wipe out the pan with a paper towel. Place it back on the heat and melt 2 tablespoons of the butter. Add the mushrooms and sauté until they begin to color, 5 to 6 minutes. Add the salt and continue to cook, stirring, for another 2 to 3 minutes, or until they are lightly browned and fully cooked. Transfer the mushrooms to the bowl with the spinach.

Turn the heat to medium-low, and place the remaining 2 tablespoons of butter in the saucepan. Add the onion and garlic and sauté for 4 to 5 minutes, or until softened. Add the flour and cook, stirring constantly, for 1 to 2 minutes. Pour in the milk and whisk until smooth. Stir in the cheese, mustard, nutmeg, and cayenne and continue to stir until the mixture is smooth and thickened. Fold in the reserved spinach and mushrooms. Taste, and adjust the seasoning with salt and black pepper.

Pour the mixture into a small ovenproof skillet or casserole dish and bake for 15 to 20 minutes, or until bubbling. Turn the oven to broil and broil for 3 to 4 minutes, or until lightly browned. Serve the dip warm.

# GOAT CHEESE—STUFFED CAPS WITH BALSAMIC-BLACKBERRY GLAZE, BURNT ONION, AND ARUGULA

Serves 2

Vegetarian

### BALSAMIC BLACKBERRY GLAZE

1/4 cup balsamic vinegar

1/2 cup blackberry preserves

1 tablespoon olive oil

1 small garlic clove, minced

1 tablespoon minced onion

Kosher salt

Freshly ground black pepper

6 to 8 large cremini mushrooms (baby bellas)

### BURNT ONIONS

2 teaspoons butter

1/2 medium sweet onion, cut into 1/4-inch slices

1 tablespoon balsamic vinegar

1/4 teaspoon sugar

Pinch of kosher salt

### GOAT CHEESE—STUFFED CAPS

3 tablespoons herbed goat cheese

2 tablespoons cream cheese

Pinch of kosher salt

2 cups baby arugula or another baby green

Fresh blackberries (optional)

*LIFE IS TOO SHORT TO STUFF A MUSHROOM. —SHIRLEY CONRAN*

Shirley may have spoken too soon! Soft goat cheese and sweet balsamic-blackberry glazed mushrooms perfectly complement the bitter salad greens, making this recipe well worth the effort. Serve with slices of grilled bread.

---

**TO MAKE THE GLAZE,** in a medium bowl, whisk together the vinegar, blackberry preserves, olive oil, garlic, and onion. Season with salt and pepper. Set aside 1/4 cup of the glaze. Remove the stems from the mushrooms (reserve and freeze for stocks). Using a fork, lightly pierce each cremini a few times. Add the mushrooms to the bowl with the glaze and gently mix until they are thoroughly covered. Let sit for at least 20 minutes or up to 3 hours (refrigerated).

**TO MAKE THE ONIONS,** in a small skillet over medium-high heat, melt the butter, add the onion slices, the vinegar, sugar, and salt and cook, stirring occasionally, for 6 to 8 minutes, or until the onions are caramelized and lightly charred. Remove from the heat.

Preheat the oven to 350 degrees F and spray a baking sheet with nonstick cooking spray.

**TO MAKE THE STUFFED CAPS,** in a small bowl, mix together the goat cheese, cream cheese, and salt. Using a teaspoon, form the mixture into 1-inch balls.

Drain the mushrooms from the marinade and spread on a baking sheet, cap sides down. Roast for 10 to 12 minutes, or until the mushrooms are cooked through. Let the mushrooms rest for 2 or 3 minutes and drain any moisture that forms in the caps. Place a small ball of the cheese mixture in each cap. Broil for 2 to 3 minutes, or until the cheese is lightly browned.

**TO SERVE,** toss the arugula with the charred onions, adding a few blackberries (if using), and spread on a serving platter. Arrange the stuffed mushroom caps on top and drizzle with the reserved marinade.

# PETITE APPLEWOOD-SMOKED PORTOBELLO CROQUE MONSIEUR

### MORNAY SAUCE

2 tablespoons butter

2 tablespoons all-purpose flour

1 1/2 cups whole milk

1/2 teaspoon kosher salt

1/4 teaspoon freshly ground
   black pepper

1/4 teaspoon ground nutmeg

1 teaspoon fresh thyme leaves

1 cup grated white cheddar
   cheese

### CROQUE MONSIEUR

2 teaspoons cider jelly

2 tablespoons Dijon mustard

2 tablespoons applewood chips

Smoking skillet (see page 20)

4 portobello mushroom caps,
   stemmed and cut into
   1/4-inch-thick slices

2 tablespoons red wine

1 tablespoon soy sauce

Pinch of sugar

2 tablespoons butter

8 (1/2-inch-thick) slices large
   French baguette

1 1/2 cups grated white cheddar
   cheese

Smoked portobello mushrooms sautéed in red wine and a splash of soy, are topped with a luxurious white cheddar Mornay sauce and sweet cider-mustard, creating a unique and delicious Croque Monsieur. They may be small, but these little French sandwiches are rich and full of flavor.

For a Croque Madame add a soft-fried egg on top. Serve with a frisée salad or some mixed fruit.

---

**TO MAKE THE MORNAY SAUCE,** melt the butter in a small saucepan over medium-low heat. Whisk in the flour and cook, whisking often, for 1 to 2 minutes. Slowly pour the milk into the saucepan and whisk until smooth. Add the salt, pepper, nutmeg, and thyme and continue to cook, whisking often, for 4 to 5 minutes, or until the sauce has thickened. Stir in the cheese, stir or whisk until smooth, and remove from the heat. Cover and set aside.

**TO MAKE THE CROQUE MONSIEUR,** in a small bowl, stir together the cider jelly and mustard and set aside.

Add the applewood chips to the smoking skillet and heat over high until the chips are smoking. Place the mushrooms on the rack, cover, and smoke for 2 minutes. Remove the mushrooms from the skillet.

Place a medium saucepan over medium-high heat, pour in the wine, soy sauce, and sugar, and bring to a simmer. Stir in the butter, add the mushroom slices, and cook for 5 to 6 minutes, or until the liquid has mostly been absorbed and the mushrooms are glazed and beginning to crisp. Transfer the mushrooms to a plate.

Preheat the oven to 425 degrees F.

Spread a thin layer of the mustard-jelly mixture on 4 of the baguette slices. Place one-fourth of the mushrooms on each slice of bread and top each with 1/4 cup of cheese. Close with the remaining 4 baguette slices. Generously spread the mornay sauce on the top of each sandwich and sprinkle evenly with the remaining 1/2 cup of cheese. Place the sandwiches on a baking sheet and bake for 5 to 6 minutes, or until the interior cheese is melted. Turn the oven to broil, and broil until the tops are lightly browned. Serve immediately.

# ORECCHIETTE WITH CREMINI AND CHERRY TOMATOES

Serves 4

Vegetarian

12 ounces dry orecchiette

3 tablespoons olive oil, divided

8 ounces cremini mushrooms, stems trimmed and quartered (about 3 1/2 cups)

1/2 teaspoon kosher salt, plus more as needed

1/2 pint cherry tomatoes or grape tomatoes, halved

Pinch of red pepper flakes

1/3 cup dry wine

4 ounces fontina cheese, grated (about 1 cup)

Freshly ground black pepper

3 tablespoons chopped fresh basil leaves

You will love this simple, light, and cheesy, summer pasta dish filled with ripe cherry tomatoes and fresh herbs. Throw the fontina in the freezer while prepping the other ingredients for easier grating.

In a large pot over high heat, bring lightly salted water to a boil. Add the orecchiette and cook for 7 to 8 minutes, or until al dente. Reserve 1 cup of the pasta water and set it aside. Drain the pasta.

Heat 2 tablespoons of the olive oil in a large saucepan over medium-high heat. Add the mushrooms and cook, 4 to 5 minutes, or until beginning to color. Add the salt and continue to cook for another 3 to 4 minutes, or until the mushrooms are lightly browned and cooked through. Add the remaining 1 tablespoon of olive oil, stir in the tomatoes and the pepper flakes, and sauté for 1 to 2 minutes. Pour in the wine and cook until the wine is reduced by half. Add the pasta and toss until coated with the mushrooms and tomatoes. Fold in the cheese, add 1/2 cup of the reserved pasta water, a little at a time, and continue to toss and stir until the cheese has just begun to melt and the ingredients are combined. Add more water if necessary. Taste, and adjust the seasoning with salt and pepper. Stir in the basil and serve.

# PORTOBELLO MUSHROOM VINAIGRETTE

Makes about ¾ cup

Vegan

1 roasted or grilled portobello
   mushroom or 3 cremini
   mushrooms
¼ cup balsamic vinegar
½ teaspoon Dijon mustard
½ cup olive oil
Kosher salt
Freshly ground black pepper

This versatile mushroom dressing, easy to prepare and loaded with umami flavor, was inspired by the late, legendary chef, Charlie Trotter. The portobellos add a nice earthy flavor and texture, though porcini, shiitake, or cremini mushrooms would work well too. Try a spoonful over a grilled steak or a spinach salad with crumbles of soft goat or blue cheese. Double or triple the recipe for a crowd. Extra dressing can be stored for up to 1 week in the refrigerator in an airtight container.

Combine the portobello, vinegar, mustard, and olive oil in a food processor or blender, and purée until smooth. Taste, and season with salt and pepper.

# DUXELLES

Duxelles (duk-SELL), are useful in many dishes, they freeze beautifully, and are one of the very best methods for preserving fresh mushrooms. Pull some out of the freezer and use in a ragu, a soup, on burgers or crostini, over pasta, on baked potatoes, or in a vegetarian lasagna. Endless possibilities!

Use only fresh mushrooms, dense button type or caps work best, but almost any mushroom will do. Keep the seasoning simple, you'll then be able to alter the taste to suit intended dishes later. A little bit of extra fat helps shield the duxelles from freezer burn. Store them in airtight freezer bags or covered ice trays.

---

**1 pound button, cremini, or assorted mushrooms of choice, cleaned and trimmed**

**4 tablespoons butter or good olive oil**

**1 shallot, minced**

**$\frac{3}{4}$ teaspoon kosher salt**

**Freshly ground black pepper**

**Olive oil (optional)**

In a food processor or by hand, pulse or mince the mushrooms until they are in $\frac{1}{8}$- to $\frac{1}{4}$-inch pieces, being careful not to chop them too fine.

Heat the butter in a large sauté pan over medium heat. Add the shallot and cook, stirring, for 2 to 3 minutes, or until softened. Stir in the mushrooms and season with salt and pepper. Cook, stirring often, until the mushrooms have given up and reabsorbed their liquid, are a golden brown, and almost dry, 7 to 8 minutes. If not using right away, stir in a drizzle of olive oil, transfer to an airtight container, and freeze for up to 4 months.

# MUSHROOM WELLINGTON WITH HERBED CHÈVRE AND MADEIRA SAUCE

Serves 2

Vegetarian option

**WELLINGTON**

4 (5-inch) portobello mushroom caps, stems and excess gills removed

2 tablespoons olive oil

½ teaspoon kosher salt, plus more as needed

½ cup Duxelles (page 57)

¼ cup ground walnuts

¼ cup finely chopped fresh spinach

2 tablespoons brandy

Freshly ground black pepper

2 tablespoons herbed goat cheese

4 thin slices prosciutto (optional)

1 egg

1 tablespoon water

2 sheets frozen puff pastry, thawed

This twist on the English classic, and an impressive company dish, uses portobello caps, though any large cap will do (wine caps would be a perfect substitute). The roasted caps are filled with herbed goat cheese surrounded by spinach, walnuts, and duxelles. The mushrooms are then wrapped in prosciutto and puff pastry and baked. The mushrooms can be stuffed, and the sauce made a day ahead. Omit the prosciutto for a vegetarian option. Make just half the filling and exchange the portobellos for shiitake or smaller caps to create an elegant appetizer.

An additional lattice of pastry is a nice touch and can be easily made with a lattice roller—available online or in most cooking stores.

---

Preheat the oven to 425 degrees F.

**TO MAKE THE WELLINGTON,** brush the mushroom caps on both sides with the olive oil and sprinkle with the salt. Place them on the baking sheet, gill sides up, and roast for 5 to 6 minutes, or until the caps are just tender. Let them rest for a few minutes and blot any liquid released from the caps with paper towels. You'll want them to be dry when you stuff them.

In a saucepan over medium heat, combine the duxelles, walnuts, spinach, and brandy and cook, stirring often, for 3 to 4 minutes, or until the mixture is cooked through and dry. Season with salt and pepper. Set aside to cool.

Evenly spread half of the duxelles mixture onto the gill sides of 2 of the mushroom caps. Form the goat cheese into 2 even-size small balls, and place 1 in each duxelles-filled cap. Cover the cheese with the remaining duxelles mixture, and place the remaining mushroom caps, cup sides down, on top of each, gently pressing to close completely. Remove any excess duxelles. Wrap each filled mushroom with a prosciutto slice and refrigerate until ready to cook.

Line a baking sheet with parchment paper.

## MADEIRA SAUCE

1 cup Mushroom Demi-Glace (page 233) or commercial vegetable or veal demi-glace

2 tablespoons Madeira

Kosher salt

Freshly ground black pepper

1 tablespoon chilled butter, cut into thirds

In a small bowl, make an egg wash by whisking the egg and water.

Roll out each sheet of puff pastry and cut into 2 (7-inch) squares. Reserve any leftover puff pastry to use for decoration. Place 1 filled mushroom in the center of 1 puff pastry square and fold over the pastry until it's fully enclosed. Trim off any excess dough. Turn it over and pat down the enclosed mushroom to form a nice round shape. Repeat with the remaining stuffed mushroom and puff pastry. Place the pastry-wrapped mushrooms on the prepared baking sheet, smooth sides up, and brush with the egg wash. Decorate the tops with half-circle cuts using the metal end of a pastry bag, or another design of your choosing from the leftover pastry.

Bake for 20 to 25 minutes, or until the Wellingtons are a nice golden brown. Remove from the oven to cool.

Make the sauce while the Wellingtons are baking.

**TO MAKE THE MADEIRA SAUCE**, in a small saucepan over medium-low heat, bring the demi-glace to a simmer. Stir in the Madeira and cook for 5 to 6 minutes, taste, and adjust the seasoning with salt and pepper. Remove from the heat and whisk in the chilled butter, 1 piece at a time.

Serve the Wellingtons with the Madeira sauce.

# CANDY CAP
*Lactarius rubidus*

# WHO WOULD HAVE THOUGHT mushrooms could be used in desserts? Or cocktails? Deeply maple-scented when dried, candy cap mushrooms are delicious in both. A variety of Lactarius, commonly known as milk cap, these unique and unusual mushrooms primarily can be found growing along the West Coast in California, Oregon, and Washington. Of all the milk caps, the candy cap is the most abundant. The mushroom growing season is mid-fall through winter, but dried candy caps can be found year-round.

## NUTRITIONAL VALUE

Candy cap mushrooms contain B vitamins such as thiamine, riboflavin, and folate, which contribute to overall brain health. They are low in calories and high in fiber and protein.

## SELECTION AND STORAGE

If you're foraging for these mushrooms, look for younger mushrooms, those with convex caps and few spots or bug damage. You're most likely to find the dried variety online, and they tend to be expensive, but they are readily available. Drying is the optimum method for preserving these mushrooms should you find a fair quantity of fresh ones. Appropriately stored in airtight containers, they will stay fragrant for years.

## COOKING METHODS

Add to braising liquids and syrups, dry them for powders, sauté

## CULINARY TIPS

Although prized for their unique and highly intense maple flavor when they are dried, they are only faintly aromatic when fresh. Slow dehydration produces a strong, burnt caramel-like fragrance. The dried mushrooms can be ground into a powder, steeped in cream to make flans or brûlées, or used to create glazes or sauces for savory dishes, including game, pork, or duck. After steeping candy caps in melted sugar, a sweet maple-like syrup can easily be made to flavor cookies and cakes, ice cream, or cocktails.

## FLAVOR PAIRINGS

| | | | |
|---|---|---|---|
| • Almonds | • Cream | • Nuts | • Turkey |
| • Anise | • Curry | • Pears | • Vanilla |
| • Bananas | • Duck | • Pecans | • Walnuts |
| • Blueberries | • Figs | • Pork | |
| • Bourbon | • Game | • Pumpkin | |
| • Coconut | • Ham | • Rum | |

# CANDY CAP SIMPLE SYRUP AND CANDIED CANDY CAPS

Makes ¾ cup

Vegan

1½ cups water

5 grams (approximately ¼ cup) dried candy cap mushrooms

1 cup packed brown sugar, muscovado sugar, or granulated sugar, plus more for sprinkling

This easy simple syrup will be a sweet addition to almost any dessert or cocktail, whenever you want to add an intense, maple-burnt caramel flavor that only candy caps provide. My favorite part of the recipe is the added bonus of the dried mushrooms remaining after you make the syrup. Once strained, they bake up into crunchy candy that can be sprinkled whole on ice cream, added to cookie recipes, or sprinkled on desserts.

In a saucepan over low heat, combine the water and the mushrooms and simmer for about 20 minutes, or until the liquid is reduced to 1 cup. Stir in the sugar, bring back to a simmer, and continue to cook for an additional 8 to 10 minutes, or until the syrup coats the back of a spoon. Strain well, reserving the mushrooms.

Preheat the oven to 350 degrees F. Line a baking sheet with parchment paper.

Place the mushroom pieces on the baking sheet and toss with a healthy sprinkle of sugar. Bake for 12 to 15 minutes, or until crisp. They will continue to crisp up after removing them from the oven.

Let cool and store in an airtight container at room temperature. The syrup can be stored in the refrigerator for up to 6 months.

# CANDY CAP
# CREAM MARTINI

1 egg white

Maple sugar or granulated
   sugar, for the rim

3 ounces vodka

½ ounce brandy

½ ounce Candy Cap Simple
   Syrup (page 62)

½ ounce heavy cream

A perfect dessert martini! Rimming the glass with egg white before dipping it in sugar makes a solidly coated sugar rim.

Place the egg white in a shallow bowl or saucer and pour the sugar into a separate saucer. Dip the rims of two martini glasses first in the egg white and then in the sugar. Let dry for 1 to 2 minutes before making the cocktail.

Fill a mixing glass or cocktail shaker with ice. Add the vodka, brandy, candy cap syrup, and cream and shake until well mixed. Strain and pour into the martini glasses.

# CANDY CAP
# SALTED BUTTER

1 cup butter, at room
   temperature

5 tablespoons Candy Cap Simple
   Syrup (page 62)

1 teaspoon flaked sea salt

This salty-sweet butter spread is perfect for biscuits, homemade rolls, or bread, with the added health benefits of mushrooms. Try it on banana bread, or use it to glaze carrots, sweet potatoes, or squash.

In a medium bowl using a hand mixer, cream the butter. Add the syrup and salt and beat until combined. Store the butter in a covered container in the refrigerator for up to 10 days.

# CANDY CAP GRANOLA

3 cups old-fashioned rolled oats

²/₃ cup almonds

¹/₂ cup pistachios

¹/₂ teaspoon kosher salt

¹/₂ teaspoon ground cinnamon

¹/₃ cup Candy Cap Simple Syrup
(page 62)

¹/₃ cup Candied Candy Caps
(page 62) chopped
(optional)

¹/₃ cup coconut oil

¹/₂ cup chopped dried apricots

Almonds, pistachios, dried apricots, and candy cap syrup make a delicious and healthy granola. Improvise by using different nuts and dried fruits. Crumble over your favorite Greek yogurt for a nice breakfast or snack.

Preheat the oven to 300 degrees F. Line a baking sheet with parchment paper.

In a large bowl, combine the oats, almonds, pistachios, salt, and cinnamon and stir until blended. Add the candy cap syrup, candy caps (if using), and coconut oil and mix very thoroughly. Transfer the mixture to the baking sheet and spread it out evenly with a spatula or large spoon.

Bake for 15 minutes. Remove from the oven and stir in the dried apricots. Using a spatula, press down on the granola to make an even layer. Return to the oven and bake for an additional 10 to 15 minutes, or until the granola is lightly golden.

Let cool for at least 45 minutes—if you can resist! Break into pieces and enjoy.

# CANDY CAP CRÈME BRÛLÉE

2 cups heavy cream

1/2 ounce dried candy caps
(about 1/2 cup)

1/2 cup granulated sugar

1/8 teaspoon kosher salt

6 egg yolks

1/3 cup maple sugar

The first time I smelled dried candy caps, I was completely smitten. The aroma of maple is intense, with hints of savory in the background. Mixing the mushroom essence into creamy sweet custard with a crunchy, burnt maple sugar topping makes an irresistible, classic dessert. Steeping the dried candy caps first in the cream adds a twist of mushroom, with that amazing maple flavor.

Preheat the oven to 325 degrees F.

In a medium saucepan over medium heat, stir together the cream and the candy caps and bring just to a boil. Remove from the heat, cover the pan, and let steep and cool for 15 minutes.

In a large bowl, whisk together the granulated sugar, salt, and egg yolks. Strain the warm cream and whisk it into the egg mixture, about 1/2 cup at a time, continuing to whisk until all the cream has been added.

Place 4 (6-ounce) ramekins in a large baking dish or roasting pan. Divide the custard mixture equally into the ramekins. Pour hot water into the baking dish until it reaches halfway up the sides of the ramekins.

Bake for 35 to 45 minutes, or until just set. The custard should still be jiggly. Carefully remove the ramekins and refrigerate for at least 2 hours. (At this point the custards can be covered and kept in the refrigerator for up to 3 days.)

When ready to serve, sprinkle the maple sugar evenly over the tops of the custards. Using a small kitchen torch, caramelize the sugar until dark brown and bubbly. (Alternatively, you can place the ramekins on a baking sheet and broil until the sugar is caramelized. Let the custards rest for a few minutes to set up and serve.)

# CAULIFLOWER (SPARASSIS)

*Sparassis crispa*

# CAULIFLOWER MUSHROOMS are one of the most delicious, foraged mushrooms

you'll find—if you're lucky! The cauliflower mushroom, also known as Sparassis, is an elusive mushroom. You'll maybe spot them while mushroom hunting if you're here in the U.S. on either the East or West Coast. Look for them growing at the base of pine trees on dead or dying roots. Known for their culinary and medicinal benefits, they are also popular throughout Europe and Asia. They are now being cultivated in multiple countries and are occasionally exported to the States, so you may one day discover Sparassis in your local supermarket.

These unique, beautiful, and delicious mushrooms, named for their lacy cream-colored cauliflower-like appearance, have a mild flavor and are some of the healthiest mushrooms you can eat. One of my personal favorites, they are the ultimate soup mushroom. Their taste and texture resemble an al dente egg noodle, and they readily absorb the flavors of the stocks they are simmered in.

## NUTRITIONAL VALUE
Another superfood mushroom, recent studies suggest that cauliflower mushrooms contain natural chemicals that boost the immune system and have antitumor, antiviral, and biological properties. They also may protect against heart disease, act as an anti-inflammatory, and help treat diabetes and staph infections.

## SELECTION AND STORAGE
Select or harvest younger mushrooms that are lighter in color. Avoid ones with yellow or decaying lobes. Their dense, almost lacy, structure captures dirt and bugs. You'll need to wash and thoroughly dry them before storing. They should last in the refrigerator for several days wrapped in paper towels in a partially open plastic storage bag. Cauliflower mushrooms can be dried for long-term storage and they freeze well after blanching them in salted water.

## COOKING METHODS
Braise, broil, fry, roast, sauté

## CULINARY TIPS
Cauliflower mushrooms hold their texture well in long braises and are healthy to fry or sauté since they don't readily absorb butter and oils like most other mushrooms. They are a good stand-in for noodles in most soups or casseroles. They also can be fried or roasted and crisp up nicely. Their flavor is mild but woodsy and they pair well with seafood and poultry.

## FLAVOR PAIRINGS

- Asian cuisine
- Bacon
- Basil
- Broth
- Butter
- Carrots
- Celery
- Cheese: Asiago, Parmesan
- Chicken
- Crab
- Cream
- Duck
- Eggplant
- Eggs
- Fennel
- Garlic
- Onions
- Parsley
- Pork
- Sorrel
- Tarragon
- Thyme

# WHITE BEAN RIBOLLITA WITH CAULIFLOWER MUSHROOMS

4 tablespoons olive oil, divided, plus more as needed

½ onion, finely chopped

1 large carrot, diced

1 large celery stalk, diced

3 garlic cloves, finely chopped

1 teaspoon kosher salt, plus more as needed

1 tablespoon double-concentrated tomato paste

Pinch of red pepper flakes

1 (14-ounce) can cannellini beans, drained, or 1½ cups cooked dried beans, divided

3½ cups chicken or vegetable stock, divided

1 (14-ounce) can plum tomatoes

4 ounces cauliflower mushrooms, torn into 1- to 2-inch pieces (about 2 cups)

2 cups fresh kale or spinach, torn into 2-inch pieces

¼ cup fresh basil leaves

2 thyme sprigs

1 (2-inch) Parmesan rind

Freshly ground black pepper

2 cups (2- to 3-inch pieces) sourdough bread

½ cup grated Parmesan cheese, divided

Ribollita, a Tuscan bean soup, thickened with crusty, toasted bread, is a favorite of mine. Cauliflower mushrooms are a welcome addition. Pour a nice glass of red wine, get cozy, and enjoy!

Heat 2 tablespoons olive oil in a Dutch oven or soup pot over medium heat. Add the onion and sauté for 5 to 6 minutes until translucent. Add the carrot, celery, garlic, and the salt and continue to cook for an additional 10 to 12 minutes, or until the vegetables are tender. Stir in the tomato paste and pepper flakes and continue to cook for an additional 1 to 2 minutes, until the tomato paste darkens in color. Remove from the heat.

In a blender, purée ⅓ cup of the beans with ½ cup of the stock. Return the pot to the stovetop, and over medium-low heat, add the bean purée along with the tomatoes, crushing them with a wooden spoon. Stir in the mushrooms, the kale, the remaining beans, remaining 3 cups of stock, and add the basil, thyme sprigs, and the Parmesan rind. Cook at a slow simmer, for 20 to 25 minutes, stirring occasionally, until the soup has thickened and the vegetables are tender. Season with salt and pepper to taste.

Preheat the oven to 350 degrees F.

While the soup is cooking, in a medium bowl, toss the bread with the remaining 2 tablespoons of olive oil, ¼ cup of Parmesan cheese, and salt to taste. Spread the bread evenly on a baking sheet and bake for 6 to 8 minutes, or until the bread is golden and crisp.

Taste the soup and adjust the seasoning with additional salt and black pepper if necessary and remove the thyme sprigs and the Parmesan rind. Fold the bread pieces into the soup. Top with the remaining Parmesan cheese and serve.

# CAULIFLOWER MUSHROOM KIMCHI

5 to 6 cups roughly chopped trimmed cauliflower mushrooms (about 12 ounces)

1 carrot, cut into matchsticks

4 green onions, green parts only, trimmed and cut into 1-inch pieces

1 1/2 teaspoons grated peeled fresh ginger

3 garlic cloves

1 1/2 tablespoons Korean red pepper flakes

1 teaspoon fish sauce

2 teaspoons rice wine vinegar

1/2 teaspoon granulated sugar

1/4 cup unsweetened pear or apple juice, plus more as needed

Cauliflower mushrooms, with their cabbage-like texture and mild flavor, are well suited for kimchi. This kimchi is easy to prepare and ready to serve within an hour, although the flavor improves after a day or two. Spicy, citrusy Korean red pepper flakes are pretty much essential for true kimchi, and a good versatile dried chile to have on hand.

Bring a medium pot of salted water to a boil over high heat. Add the chopped mushrooms and boil for 2 to 3 minutes. Transfer the mushrooms to a bowl using a slotted spoon. Add the carrot to the pot and simmer for 1 minute. Transfer the carrot to the bowl with the mushrooms, add the green onions, and stir until combined. Reserve 1 cup of the boiling water and set aside.

Using a food processor or blender, combine the ginger, garlic, pepper flakes, fish sauce, vinegar, sugar, and pear juice and blend into a loose paste, adding more pear juice if necessary.

Add the paste to the bowl with the vegetables, and using your hands or a spoon, toss the mixture until thoroughly coated. Pack the mixture in jars or a glass container with a lid and add some of the reserved cooking water to cover the kimchi. The kimchi will keep in the refrigerator for several weeks as long as the vegetables are covered with liquid.

# SHRIMP AND CAULIFLOWER MUSHROOM EGG ROLLS

1 tablespoon peanut, grapeseed, or canola oil, plus more for frying

1 garlic clove, minced

1/2 teaspoon minced peeled fresh ginger

3 ounces thinly sliced cauliflower mushrooms (about 1 1/2 cups)

1 cup thinly sliced Napa cabbage

1/2 cup shredded carrot

2 teaspoons soy sauce, plus more for serving

2 teaspoons Shaoxing wine or mirin

1/2 teaspoon sesame oil

8 ounces raw shrimp, cleaned and finely chopped

1/2 cup bean sprouts

2 green onions, green parts only, finely chopped

Kosher salt

1 egg

1 tablespoon water

8 to 10 egg roll wrappers

Sweet chili sauce, for serving

Cauliflower mushrooms have a leafy texture, absorb flavors well, and make a great filling for egg rolls. Serve with sweet chili sauce or your favorite dipping sauce.

Heat the peanut oil in a large skillet over medium-low heat. Add the garlic and ginger and sauté for about 2 minutes, or until softened.

Raise the heat to medium, stir in the mushrooms, cabbage, and carrot and cook, stirring often, for an additional 3 to 4 minutes, or until the vegetables are barely tender. Stir in the soy sauce, wine, and sesame oil. Add the shrimp and cook for 1 to 2 minutes, or until opaque.

Remove the pan from the heat, add the bean sprouts and green onions, and toss to thoroughly combine. Taste, and adjust the seasoning with salt.

In a small bowl, mix the egg with the water.

Place 1 tablespoon of the filling mixture on the lower half of an egg roll wrapper. Roll the bottom edge up and over the mixture, fold in the sides, and continue to roll, using the egg wash to seal the edges. Repeat for the rest of the filling and wrappers.

In a large skillet over medium-high heat, bring 2 to 3 inches of peanut oil to 350 degrees F. Add the egg rolls and fry, turning occasionally, for 3 to 4 minutes, or until golden brown and crispy. Serve with sweet chili sauce.

# CHANTERELLE
## *Cantharellus*

**CHANTERELLES** are famous worldwide for good reason. They are among the most beautiful, and arguably, one of the tastiest mushroom species. And luckily for all of us, they grow in one variety or another globally. They range in size and color from tiny red cinnabars to larger golden and even white varieties, making them easy to spot.

You'll find them emerging from the soil in shaded areas when rain and warm temperatures combine. They'll start to pop up along the East Coast and in the South and Midwest from June through September; the season is later on the West Coast and in the Pacific Northwest, and generally ranges from fall through January.

### NUTRITIONAL VALUE

Chanterelles, along with morels, contain the highest amount of vitamin D of any mushroom, between 60 to 100 percent of your daily recommended intake per cup. Vitamin D is an anti-inflammatory, significant for older individuals as well as for vegans and vegetarians who may need more plant-based sources of this critical vitamin. They are also a good source of B and C vitamins, copper, potassium, selenium, manganese, iron, and phosphorus.

## SELECTION AND STORAGE

Look for chanterelles with flatter caps; their edges turn under as they age and begin to wilt. Avoid those that have brown spots or spongy stems. Choose mushrooms that smell fruity, like apricots or fresh squash or pumpkin.

As with all mushrooms, clean them before storing or cooking. A good wipe with a paper towel or a swipe with a mushroom brush should suffice. If they are freshly foraged and likely dirty, the mushrooms can be lightly rinsed. Pat or air-dry them before cooking.

Thankfully, these beautiful mushrooms keep longer than most (particularly the white and golden varieties) and can be held in the refrigerator if stored properly for up to 10 days. Wrap them loosely in paper towels and store them in a paper bag on the bottom shelf.

Freezing is another option, especially if you're lucky and have a large bounty. Chanterelles are best if they are cooked before freezing; sauté them first in butter or oil and store the mushrooms, lightly covered in the fat, in an airtight bag or container before freezing. Or dry sauté the mushrooms over medium-low heat, pat dry, let cool completely, and store them in a vacuum-sealed or regular freezer bag with the air pressed out and freeze. Alternatively, you can freeze them raw on a baking sheet until solid and place them in the freezer in airtight containers. Any of these freezing methods will preserve the mushrooms for 2 months or longer.

Pickling is another method to consider. Chanterelles are delicious in a conserve, and you'll have them to enjoy for many months.

Drying chanterelles is generally not recommended since they will lose too much flavor.

## COOKING METHODS

Bake, pickle, roast, sauté

## CULINARY TIPS

One of the best ways for chanterelle mushrooms to be savored is after a quick sauté in butter with a splash of lemon juice and maybe a sprinkle of fresh herbs. Serve them as a stand-alone side dish or drench them in cream and brandy over toasted brioche for a more substantial main dish. They are simply delicious in eggs and make a dramatic presentation spooned on top of a perfectly grilled steak.

## FLAVOR PAIRINGS

- Beef
- Butter
- Cheese, Parmesan
- Corn
- Cream
- Eggs
- Garlic
- Honey
- Oil, olive
- Onions
- Parsley
- Pasta
- Peas
- Potatoes
- Poultry
- Shallots
- Soups
- Thyme
- Vinegar, sherry
- Wine, white

# ENGLISH PEAS WITH CHANTERELLES AND SHALLOTS

Serves 4

Vegetarian

2 tablespoons butter, divided

1 extra-large or 2 medium shallots, cut into ¼-inch-thick slices lengthwise

Pinch of granulated sugar

3 ounces chanterelle mushrooms cleaned, trimmed, and thinly sliced (about 1½ cups)

½ teaspoon kosher salt, plus more as needed

2 cups cooked fresh peas or thawed frozen peas

2 tablespoons heavy cream (optional)

1 tablespoon chopped fresh basil

Freshly ground black pepper

Peas and mushrooms are a classic combination. In this recipe, golden chanterelles replace the usual button mushrooms, with caramelized shallots adding a sweet note to the dish. Use fresh peas if you can find them. Finish with a couple tablespoons of cream for a further indulgence if you like.

Heat 1 tablespoon of the butter in a large skillet over medium heat. Add the shallot and sugar and cook for 6 to 8 minutes, or until the shallot is caramelized and tender. Transfer the shallot to a plate.

Add the remaining 1 tablespoon of butter to the skillet, stir in the mushrooms, and sauté, adding the salt halfway through the cooking time, for 8 to 10 minutes, or until lightly caramelized.

Add the peas and the reserved shallot and toss thoroughly with the mushrooms. Drizzle in the cream (if using). Stir in the basil and cook for 3 to 4 minutes, or until the peas are heated through. Be careful not to overcook.

Taste, and adjust the seasoning with salt and pepper.

# CHANTERELLE-APRICOT GALETTE WITH ARMAGNAC AND VANILLA CRÈME FRAÎCHE

Serves 4 to 6

Vegetarian

## VANILLA CRÈME FRAÎCHE

1 cup crème fraîche

Scraped seeds from ½ vanilla
    bean

1 tablespoon honey

## GALETTE

3 tablespoons butter

4 ounces chanterelles, cut into
    ¼- to ½-inch slices (about
    2 cups)

3 tablespoons apricot preserves

1 tablespoon Armagnac or
    brandy

¼ teaspoon ground cinnamon

2 tablespoons granulated sugar

½ teaspoon kosher salt

¼ teaspoon freshly ground
    black pepper

1 sheet pie dough

1 large egg

1 tablespoon water

Raw sugar or turbinado sugar,
    for sprinkling

¼ cup sliced almonds
    (optional)

You'll love presenting this dessert to your guests—they won't believe it's made with mushrooms! Chanterelles, with their slightly citrusy flavor and mild apricot aroma, are tossed with butter and apricot preserves, hit with a splash of brandy, briefly cooked, and baked in a flaky pie crust topped with vanilla crème fraîche. Ice cream would be equally delicious.

(Use your favorite pie dough recipe or Cynthia's Pie Crust (page 179), halve the recipe for one galette and add one tablespoon of sugar to the ingredients.) If you're short on time, use a high quality store-bought pie dough.

---

**TO MAKE THE CRÈME FRAÎCHE,** in a small bowl, whisk together the crème fraîche, vanilla seeds, and honey. Cover and keep chilled in the refrigerator until serving.

Preheat the oven to 400 degrees F. Line a baking sheet with parchment paper.

**TO MAKE THE GALETTE,** in a medium saucepan over medium heat, melt the butter. Add the mushrooms, preserves, Armagnac, cinnamon, granulated sugar, salt, and pepper and cook, stirring often, for 2 to 3 minutes, or until the mushrooms are just beginning to release their liquid. Remove the pan from the heat.

On a clean, floured work surface, roll out the pie dough to a 12-inch circle. Place the dough on the prepared baking sheet and spread the mushroom mixture in the center, leaving a 1½-inch border of dough. Fold the dough border over the edges of the filling, and pinch into pleats. Press gently to seal. Mix the egg and water together in a small bowl. Brush the dough edges with the egg wash and sprinkle with the raw sugar. Top with sliced almonds (if using). Bake for 20 to 25 minutes, or until the crust is golden brown. Let cool. Serve topped with the crème fraîche.

# CHANTERELLES ON CARAMELIZED BRIOCHE

3 tablespoons butter, divided, plus more as needed

2 thick slices brioche

2 medium shallots, thinly sliced crosswise

8 ounces fresh chanterelle mushrooms, trimmed and halved lengthwise (about 3 1/2 cups)

Kosher salt

Freshly ground black pepper

3 tablespoons brandy

1/3 cup heavy cream

2 tablespoons finely chopped fresh herbs, such as parsley, chives, or tarragon, divided

Here's a decadent update on the British classic—mushrooms on toast. Fresh chanterelles are sautéed in butter then finished with a splash of brandy and heavy cream. They are then served over skillet-caramelized brioche and sprinkled with fresh herbs. Perfect for brunch.

Heat 1 tablespoon of the butter in a large skillet over medium heat. Place the brioche slices in the skillet and cook for 2 to 3 minutes, turning once, or until golden brown on both sides. Transfer to a plate and keep warm.

Add another tablespoon of butter to the skillet. Stir in the shallots and sauté for 4 to 5 minutes, or until softened and lightly caramelized. Remove to a plate. Add the remaining 1 tablespoon of butter to the skillet and, working in batches, if necessary, sauté the mushrooms for 8 to 10 minutes, or until golden and crispy. Season the mushrooms midway through cooking with salt and pepper. You may need to add more butter if cooking in batches. Add the shallots back to the pan with the brandy, the heavy cream, and 1 tablespoon of the fresh herbs. Bring to a simmer and cook for 4 to 5 minutes, or until thickened. Remove from the heat, taste, and adjust the seasoning with salt and pepper.

Spoon the mushroom sauce over the brioche slices and garnish with the remaining fresh herbs.

# CHANTERELLES AND HERBED FREGOLA

Serves 2

Vegetarian

2 tablespoons olive oil

¼ cup minced shallot

1 small garlic clove, minced

1 teaspoon kosher salt, plus
   more as needed

2 ounces chanterelle mushrooms, finely chopped
   (about 1 cup)

2 tablespoons dry white wine

3 cups Roasted Mushroom
   Stock (page 232), chicken
   stock, or water

1 cup toasted fregola or Israeli
   couscous

1½ tablespoons finely chopped
   fresh parsley, divided

1 teaspoon fresh thyme leaves

Freshly ground black pepper

2 tablespoons grated Parmesan
   cheese, plus more for serving

Chanterelle mushrooms, with their nutty flavor and aroma, are right at home in a warm bowl of herbed Sardinian fregola. Fregola is a pearl-shaped, toasted semolina pasta, easily found online or in Italian food markets.

Heat the olive oil in a large saucepan over medium heat. Add the shallot, garlic, and salt and cook for 2 to 3 minutes, or until just softened. Stir in the mushrooms and sauté for 3 to 5 minutes, or until golden. Stir in the wine and cook for about 1 minute, or until the wine is mostly absorbed. Pour in the stock and bring to a simmer.

Turn the heat to medium-low, stir in the fregola, 1 tablespoon of the parsley, and the thyme leaves. Cover and cook, stirring occasionally, for about 12 minutes, or until the fregola is tender. Remove the pan from the heat, taste, and adjust the seasoning with salt and pepper. Stir in the remaining parsley and the Parmesan cheese.

Serve with additional Parmesan cheese.

# HONEY-ROASTED CHANTERELLES

²/₃ cup melted butter

¹/₃ cup honey

2 tablespoons tamari or
    low-sodium soy sauce

1 pound chanterelle mush-
    rooms, cleaned and trimmed
    (6 to 8 cups)

Kosher salt

Freshly ground black pepper

2 or 3 thyme sprigs

Honey and soy add sweetness and an added depth of flavor to roasted chanterelles. These are wonderful alongside grilled chicken or pork. Try serving them as an appetizer on toasted bread, with a dab of creamy goat cheese, or on a warm round of Brie, drizzled with a little extra honey.

Preheat the oven to 375 degrees F.

Whisk together the melted butter, honey, and tamari in a medium bowl. Add the mushrooms and toss to coat. Sprinkle with salt and pepper. Spread the mushrooms evenly on a nonstick baking sheet and scatter the thyme sprigs over them.

Roast, stirring occasionally, for 20 to 25 minutes, or until the mushrooms are caramelized and tender. Remove the thyme sprigs and serve.

# CHANTERELLE AND
# HAZELNUT PESTO

Makes about 1 1/2 cups

Vegetarian

3 to 4 tablespoons, divided, plus
  1/3 cup extra-virgin olive oil
4 ounces chanterelle
  mushrooms, trimmed and
  shredded (about 2 cups)
1 teaspoon kosher salt, plus
  more as needed
3 small garlic cloves, minced
1/2 cup toasted hazelnuts
1/2 teaspoon freshly ground
  black pepper, plus more as
  needed
1/2 cup minced fresh parsley
1/4 cup grated Parmesan cheese

Enjoy this nutty, creamy pesto tossed with pasta, spooned on a baked potato, or as an appetizer served with crackers or bread.

Heat 3 tablespoons of the olive oil in a large skillet over medium-high heat. Add the mushrooms to the skillet, toss with the oil, and cook for 6 to 8 minutes, stirring occasionally. Add the salt as the mushrooms begin to caramelize. Add more oil if necessary, until the mushrooms are cooked through. Add the garlic and cook for 1 to 2 minutes longer until softened. Transfer to a plate and cool.

In the bowl of a food processor, combine the mushrooms, hazelnuts, and pepper and pulse a couple of times until the nuts are minced and the mixture is well blended. Slowly pour in 1/3 cup of olive oil, blending until almost smooth. Add the parsley and Parmesan and pulse again until well blended. Taste and season with salt and pepper as needed.

# CHICKEN OF THE WOODS
### *Laetiporus sulphureus*

**YES, THERE ARE** chickens in the woods. And they're growing on trees! They are fungi, of course, but when you taste one that is well-prepared, you'll maybe swear it's the real thing.

Most chicken of the woods mushrooms fruit from late summer into fall, usually August through November. However, you may find some fruiting as early as June. Also known as a sulphuric polypore, you'll find these golden to bright yellow shelf-like structures growing on tree trunks and branches. Older fungi turn pale gray.

## NUTRITIONAL VALUE

Besides tasting like chicken and having a similar texture, chicken of the woods have two-thirds the amount of protein per ounce as real chicken breast meat. These mushrooms are also a good source of potassium and vitamin C and contain antioxidant, antibacterial, and anti-inflammatory properties.

## SELECTION AND STORING

If you are foraging these mushrooms, avoid those growing on conifers, eucalyptus, or hemlock. Choose younger, pale-yellow brackets, they're the best tasting and the least likely to cause stomach upset. You may find them occasionally at your local farmers' market, and they are often available online. Like all wild mushrooms, eat only in small quantities at first to ensure they sit well with you.

Wipe mushrooms clean with a damp cloth and trim away any worm-infested parts. A brief soaking in water with a little lemon juice should kill any bugs.

They will store well in the refrigerator for several days, wrapped in paper towels and placed in a paper bag. For more extended storage, freeze and store in zip-top bags with the air pressed out or vacuum seal them; they will last several months. No need to thaw them before cooking. Drying is another option—dry and store in an airtight container and you'll enjoy chicken of the woods to cook with for up to 1 year.

## COOKING METHODS

Bake, fry, pan-fry, sauté

## CULINARY USES

You can prepare these mushrooms in recipes as you would prepare chicken breast, and they are a good stand-in for chicken in a vegetarian or vegan diet. However, you may want to blanch the mushrooms at a low boil for 3 to 4 minutes, or until tender, before cooking with them. The same holds for lobster mushrooms, another bracket type of edible fungi. These mushrooms have a recommended total cooking time of 15 to 20 minutes before consuming, so a quick boil before cooking shortens your pan-finishing time, and tenderizes any tough parts of the mushroom. A pre-soak in buttermilk after blanching also helps tenderize the mushrooms and sweetens the flavor (see Buttermilk Marinade for Mushrooms on page 87).

One of the easiest and most delicious ways to prepare chicken of the woods is Milanese style; lightly breaded and pan-fried. Add a squeeze of lemon or a light tomato sauce.

These mushrooms absorb oil like a sponge, so unless you're deep-frying, be stingy with the oil.

## FLAVOR PAIRINGS

- Arugula
- Bacon
- Basil
- Bread, breadcrumbs
- Butter
- Cheese: fontina, mozzarella,

Parmesan, provolone, Romano
- Chiles
- Cilantro
- Cream
- Garlic
- Ham

- Lemon
- Olive oil
- Onions
- Pancetta
- Parsley
- Pasta
- Peppers, sweet
- Prosciutto

- Rosemary
- Sage
- Spinach
- Thyme
- Tomatoes
- Wine, white

# CHICKEN OF THE WOODS MILANESE

8 ounces chicken of the woods
    mushrooms, trimmed into
    ¼- to ½-inch-thick, palm-
    size cutlets
2 cups buttermilk
1½ cups panko breadcrumbs
¼ cup finely grated Parmesan
    cheese
½ teaspoon kosher salt, plus
    more as needed
2 eggs
2 tablespoons water
½ cup all-purpose flour
Freshly ground black pepper
Ghee, peanut, grapeseed,
    or another neutral oil, for
    pan-frying
¼ cup olive oil
⅛ cup fresh lemon juice
½ teaspoon Dijon mustard
3 cups arugula
1 cup sliced cherry tomatoes
2 tablespoons chopped fresh
    parsley
Shaved Parmesan cheese, for
    serving

Milanese sounds like it might be difficult, but it's so easy to make. The crispy breadcrumb and Parmesan cheese coating transforms the mushrooms into a company-worthy dish in just a few minutes.

Blanch the mushrooms in boiling water for 3 to 4 minutes to tenderize. Place the mushrooms in a medium bowl and pour in the buttermilk to cover. Refrigerate for at least 4 hours or overnight. (Skip this step for younger mushrooms and simply dip in the buttermilk before continuing.)

In a wide, shallow bowl, combine the panko with the Parmesan cheese, and season with the salt. In another bowl, whisk together the eggs and water to make an egg wash. Place the flour in another medium, shallow bowl.

Drain the mushrooms from the buttermilk and sprinkle them with salt and pepper. Lightly coat the mushrooms with the flour. Dip the floured mushrooms into the egg wash and then evenly coat them with the panko mixture. Set them aside on a plate.

Heat $\frac{1}{4}$ inch of ghee in an extra-large heavy skillet. Add the mushrooms and fry for 2 to 3 minutes per side until golden and crispy. Transfer the mushrooms to a plate and sprinkle lightly with salt.

In a small bowl, combine the olive oil, lemon juice, and mustard and whisk until smooth. Season with salt and pepper. Place the arugula in a medium bowl with the tomatoes, drizzle with about half of the dressing, and toss to coat. Store leftover dressing in the refrigerator.

Serve the mushrooms on a bed of arugula salad and top with chopped parsley and shaved Parmesan cheese.

# BUTTERMILK MARINADE FOR MUSHROOMS

Most mushrooms have a pleasing earthy flavor, that's why we love them, right? Some have a more intense flavor than others, and a few species like chicken of the woods and lion's mane may need a little help with mellowing their natural flavor, especially when these mushrooms are used in dishes paired with mild-flavored ingredients.

A quick soak in buttermilk will smooth out or eliminate any sour flavors your mushrooms may have. A longer soak will tenderize them as well. Buttermilk tenderizes both meat and plant-based proteins.

If you have freshly picked, younger mushrooms you may skip this step.

# BAKED CHICKEN OF THE WOODS PARMESAN WITH LEMON-BUTTER SAUCE

1 recipe Chicken of the Woods
   Milanese (page 86),
   prepared
½ cup grated Parmesan cheese,
   plus more for serving
12 ounces angel hair pasta
Olive oil, for tossing
3 tablespoons fresh lemon juice
1 cup vegetable or chicken stock
6 tablespoons cold butter, cut
   into 6 pieces
Kosher salt
Freshly ground black pepper
2 tablespoons chopped fresh
   parsley

This baked variation of Chicken of the Woods Milanese is topped with a buttery, citrusy, lemon pan sauce.

Reserve the skillet you used to make the Milanese and do not clean it.

Preheat the oven to 350 degrees F. Line a baking sheet with parchment paper.

Place the Milanese on the prepared baking sheet. Liberally sprinkle the finished cutlets with the Parmesan cheese. Bake for 3 to 4 minutes, or until the cheese has begun to melt. Transfer the cutlets to a serving platter and keep warm.

Bring a large pot of lightly salted water to a boil over high heat. Add the pasta and cook for 6 to 8 minutes, or until al dente. Drain, toss with a splash of olive oil, and transfer to a serving bowl.

Place the skillet over medium heat, pour in the lemon juice and stock, and deglaze, stirring and scraping with a spoon. Simmer for 2 to 3 minutes, or until the liquid is reduced by half. Remove the skillet from the heat and whisk in the cold butter, 1 piece at a time. Taste, and adjust the seasoning with salt and pepper. Stir in the chopped parsley.

Divide the pasta between plates or bowls and top with the cutlets and a generous spoonful of the sauce. Serve with additional grated Parmesan cheese.

# CHICKEN OF THE WOODS SALTIMBOCCA

8 ounces chicken of the woods mushrooms, trimmed into ½-inch-thick, palm-size cutlets

2 cups buttermilk

Freshly ground black pepper

8 to 10 slices prosciutto

8 to 10 fresh sage leaves

½ cup all-purpose flour

2 to 3 tablespoons olive oil

½ cup white wine

3 tablespoons cold butter

Kosher salt

Fresh lemon juice, for seasoning

Saltimbocca is a classic Italian dish that literally means "to jump in your mouth," which probably refers to its flavor or maybe to how quickly it can be made. Either way it's a keeper! Traditionally, saltimbocca is made with veal or chicken, but chicken of the woods is the star in this recipe. The mushrooms are sliced thinly, topped with prosciutto and whole sage leaves, then pan-fried until golden. A buttery wine sauce made with the pan drippings finishes the dish. Serve with your favorite pasta or polenta.

Blanch the mushrooms in lightly salted water for 3 to 4 minutes to tenderize. Place the mushrooms in a medium bowl and pour in the buttermilk to cover. Refrigerate for at least 4 hours or overnight. (Skip this step for younger mushrooms and simply dip in the buttermilk before continuing.)

Remove the mushrooms from the buttermilk marinade, keeping a light coating on the mushrooms, and season lightly with pepper.

Using a toothpick, secure 1 folded slice of prosciutto and 1 sage leaf onto the top side of each mushroom cutlet. Place the flour in a bowl, and gently press the undersides only of each cutlet in the flour to lightly coat. Set the cutlets aside on a plate.

Heat 2 tablespoons of the olive oil in a large skillet over medium heat. Working in batches, place the mushrooms in the skillet, prosciutto side down, and cook for 1 to 2 minutes, or until golden. Add the remaining tablespoon of oil if needed, turn over the cutlets (floured sides down) and cook for an additional 2 to 3 minutes, or until lightly browned and crispy. Transfer to a plate and repeat with the remaining cutlets. Keep warm.

Pour out any excess oil from the skillet and return the skillet to medium heat. Pour in the wine, deglaze the pan with a wooden spoon or spatula, scraping and stirring, and cook for 2 to 3 minutes, or until the liquid is reduced by half. Remove the skillet from the heat and whisk in the cold butter, 1 piece at a time. Taste, and adjust the seasoning with salt and pepper. Pour the sauce over the mushrooms and serve with a good hit of fresh lemon juice.

# CHICKEN OF THE WOODS TINGA

Serves 5 to 6

Vegetarian with a vegan option

3 tablespoons grapeseed or
vegetable oil

8 ounces shredded chicken
of the woods mushrooms
(3$\frac{1}{2}$ to 4 cups)

Pinch of kosher salt, plus more
as needed

1 white onion, halved and thinly
sliced lengthwise

2 garlic cloves, minced

1 cup fire-roasted crushed or
diced tomatoes

1 chipotle chile in adobo sauce,
finely chopped

1 teaspoon dried Mexican
oregano

$\frac{1}{2}$ teaspoon ground cumin

1 teaspoon granulated sugar

$\frac{1}{2}$ cup vegetable stock, water,
or chicken stock, plus more
as needed

2 tablespoons chopped fresh
cilantro

Hot sauce, for serving

Tortillas, warmed, or cooked
rice, for serving

**OPTIONAL TOPPINGS**

Cotija cheese

Sliced jalapeños

Diced red onion

Fresh cilantro

Avocado

Chicken of the woods mushrooms replace chicken in this vegetarian version of tinga, a classic Mexican-style dish usually made with shredded chicken in a tomato-adobo sauce. Tinga is usually served on a tostada, but is equally delicious over Mexican rice or as a filling for enchiladas.

Heat the oil in a large saucepan over medium heat. Add the mushrooms with a pinch of salt and sauté for 3 to 4 minutes, or until golden. Add the onion and garlic and continue to cook, stirring often, for another 2 to 3 minutes, or until the onion is softened and golden. Add the tomatoes, chile, oregano, cumin, sugar, and stock and simmer, stirring often and adding more stock as needed, for 20 to 25 minutes, or until the mushrooms are tender and the sauce has reduced and coats the mushrooms. Adjust the seasoning with salt if needed.

Stir in the cilantro and add hot sauce to taste. Serve on warm tortillas with your desired toppings.

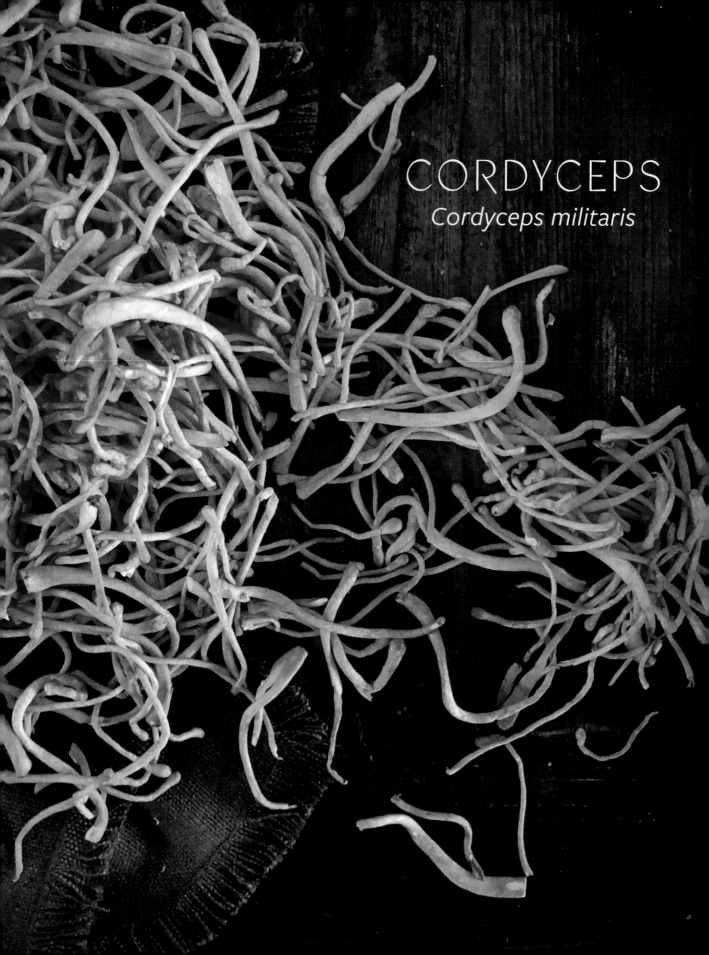

CORDYCEPS
*Cordyceps militaris*

# CORDYCEPS are a unique fungi to say the least. These alien-like, parasitic mushrooms voraciously inhabit the tissue of caterpillars and other insects with mycelium-producing spores that drain its host of nutrients, eventually replacing the host tissue before developing into mushrooms. Of the four hundred species of cordyceps growing worldwide, one variety, *Cordyceps militaris*, can easily be cultivated on a large scale on soy and rice, making it more palatable to eat, and readily available as a nutritional supplement.

## NUTRITIONAL VALUE

Cordyceps are probably best known for their health benefits. Research has shown that *Cordyceps militaris* are made of up to 35 percent beta-glucans, likely the most powerful immune system modulator in existence. In China, they are recognized for their ability to boost vitality and endurance, improve circulation, regulate blood sugar, and assist against inflammation.

Avoid eating or taking cordyceps supplements if you are on blood thinners, have problems with blood coagulation, or are scheduled to have surgery in the near future.

## COOKING METHODS

Fry, sauté, stir-fry, and use to top rice dishes or soup

## SELECTION AND STORAGE

You will likely find fresh cordyceps in Asian markets sold in commercial packaging. Leave the mushrooms stored in the refrigerator in the original packaging for the best short-term storage. Powders and tinctures are often available online for use in teas and broths.

## CULINARY USES

As bizarre as the cordyceps life cycle may seem, they are actually a pretty good eating mushroom. (No worries, the only cordyceps offered to consumers for consumption (*Cordyceps militaris*) are grown on rice—no creepy bug-eating varieties!) Their bright orange color is appealing, and their texture holds up well through a variety of cooking methods. The flavor is lightly earthy, somewhat grassy with a faint smell of squash. They can be added to soups and stews, paired with roasted meats and used in stir-fries and vegetable dishes. Deep-fried they make a nice tempura, are a good complement to creamy pasta dishes, and are a nutritious addition to sandwiches and salads.

## FLAVOR PAIRINGS

- Chicken
- Cilantro
- Dashi
- Ginger
- Leek
- Lemon
- Pasta
- Pork
- Rice
- Sesame oil
- Shallot
- Soy sauce

# CORDYCEPS KAKIAGE

Vegetable or peanut oil, for
  frying

1 whole egg

1 cup very cold water

1 cup cake flour

1 large carrot, halved and
  julienned

1 sweet onion, halved and
  separated into thin slices

3 ounces fresh cordyceps
  mushrooms (about 1½ cups)

10 to 12 green beans

Sea salt or smoked flaked salt

Fried vermicelli noodles or rice,
  for serving

Mentsuyu or dipping sauce of
  choice, for serving

A popular type of tempura in Japan, kakiage, unlike most
tempura, uses whole eggs instead of egg whites. This recipe
uses onion, carrot, and green beans along with cordyceps, but
you can substitute any vegetables you have on hand, slicing the
vegetables the same size for consistency.

Cold is the trick to good tempura batter! Use ice-cold water
and do not overmix. Serve with mentsuyu, a ready-made sauce
for tempura, that is available in Asian markets. Mentsuyu is
thick with a strong flavor; dilute with three to four parts water
or to taste.

Heat 4 inches of the oil in a heavy pot over medium-high heat to
345 degrees F.

In a medium bowl, beat the egg until smooth. Add the water and stir in
the flour to make a batter.

Stir the carrot, onion, cordyceps, and green beans into the batter. Using
tongs or a spider skimmer, gently lower the vegetables into the hot oil,
a few at a time, turning gently for 1 to 2 minutes, until crispy. Transfer
to a rack to drain, and lightly season with salt.

Serve over fried vermicelli or rice with a side of mentsuyu or your
favorite dipping sauce.

# CORDYCEPS PASTA
# AL LIMONE

12 ounces spaghetti, bucatini, or
long pasta

2 tablespoons butter or
grapeseed oil

4 ounces fresh cordyceps
mushrooms (about 2 cups)

Grated zest of $1/2$ lemon

$3/4$ cup heavy cream

$1/4$ teaspoon red pepper flakes

$1/2$ teaspoon kosher salt, plus
more as needed

$1/2$ cup grated Parmesan cheese,
plus more for serving

2 tablespoons fresh lemon juice

Freshly ground black pepper

$1/2$ cup crushed toasted walnuts

Cordyceps are a perfect fit in this classic Italian dish with their citrusy flavor and almost pasta-like consistency.

Southern Italy is famous for its delicious lemons, so it is no wonder this dish is a favorite in the region. Lemon is a star in this dish, so use only the freshest lemons! This recipe is made with cream, but it can also be made using just the starchy pasta water, or with ricotta cheese.

Bring a large pot of lightly salted water to a boil over medium-high heat, and cook the pasta for 7 to 9 minutes until al dente. Drain, reserving 1 cup of the water.

In a large saucepan over medium heat, melt the butter and sauté the cordyceps until just cooked through, 3 to 4 minutes. Transfer the cordyceps from the saucepan to a bowl.

Add the lemon zest with the cream, pepper flakes, and salt to the saucepan, bring to a simmer, and cook for 2 to 3 minutes. Stir in the cordyceps and the pasta, gently tossing to combine. Stir in the cheese, continue to toss, adding the reserved pasta water, a little at a time, until the sauce is smooth and creamy, 3 to 4 minutes. Finish by stirring in the lemon juice, then taste and season with salt and pepper.

Top with the crushed walnuts and additional grated cheese and serve.

# CORDYCEPS TEA

3 grams dried cordyceps
    mushrooms (about 10 to
    12 medium dried cordyceps)
2 cups water, plus more as
    needed

*Cordyceps militaris* is best ingested in a water-soluble form, and is highly concentrated for maximum health benefits in teas. Here is a basic recipe, and you can include additional herbs or tea leaves for increased flavor and additional vitamins. Double or triple the recipe for extra to store for later.

In a medium saucepan over medium-low heat, simmer the dried cordyceps in the water for about 45 minutes, stirring occasionally, until the mushroom's orange color fades to white. This is an indication that the mushrooms are finished dissolving all their benefits into the water.

Strain the mushrooms from the tea and add water to replace what evaporated during the long simmer. It is ready to drink when the temperature has cooled to your liking.

Refrigerate any extra tea in a jar with a tight-fitting lid. It will last for a week. Rewarm on the stove or in the microwave.

**NOTE:** You can easily incorporate the many potential health benefits of cordyceps in your diet through powders either purchased online or made from dried mushrooms. Capsules and tinctures are also available. At this time, there are no universal guidelines for an appropriate dose of cordyceps supplements. While considered generally safe, consuming them may cause stomach upset in some people.

# HEDGEHOG
*Hydnum repandum*

# HEDGEHOGS,

**HEDGEHOGS,** or "sweet tooth" mushrooms, are easy to identify and a lucky culinary find. They will surprise you with their nutty and slightly sweet flavor and woo you with their bright yellow-orange color and cute dimples. Its distinguishable tooth-like spines under the caps that make it nearly impossible to confuse with inedible and potentially poisonous look-alikes.

One edible mushroom they closely resemble is the chanterelle, only their gills set them apart. Hedgehogs share a similar but less intense flavor and have a slightly meatier texture.

You can spot hedgehog mushrooms in the fall through early winter, cuddled beneath pine, birch, and spruce trees.

## NUTRITIONAL VALUE

Hedgehogs are rich in vitamin D, potassium, and iron and like most mushrooms, they also have anti-inflammatory and antibacterial properties.

## SELECTING AND STORING

Look for dry firm mushrooms with minor bug damage and few or no damp or moldy spots.

Store in the refrigerator wrapped in paper towels and tucked into a brown paper bag.

They are not a great choice for drying, but unlike most mushrooms, they freeze well in their raw state. Simply freeze them on a sheet pan until solid and then store them in freezer bags. They will last for a few weeks, and they will thaw in perfect form. For longer freezer storage, cook them first and then seal them in airtight containers before freezing. Hedgehogs are also an ideal choice for pickling and conservas (see Wild Mushroom Conserva, page 100).

## COOKING METHODS

Bake, pickle, roast, sauté, and add to soups and stews

## COOKING TIPS

Hedgehog mushrooms are wonderful sautéed in butter with a bit of garlic and a sprinkle of chopped parsley or served alongside grilled or roasted meats or game. They hold a firm consistency and readily absorb flavors, making them a perfect addition to soups or stews, and they are a good stand-in for almost any recipe calling for chanterelles.

The tiny teeth on the underside of their caps can make them somewhat difficult to clean (a brush is handy), but the extra effort is well worth it. The tasty little spikes will detach during cooking and leave tiny, flavorful bits floating in your sauce or broth. If your recipe calls for a clear sauce or soup, choose another mushroom or remove the spikes with the edge of a spoon or sharp knife before cooking.

## FLAVOR PAIRINGS

- Apple
- Basil
- Brandy
- Butter
- Corn
- Cream
- Garlic
- Honey
- Lemon
- Olive oil
- Parsley
- Pepper, black
- Pine nuts
- Sherry, dry
- Thyme
- Tomatoes, sun-dried
- Vinegar: sherry, white wine

# WILD MUSHROOM CONSERVA

Makes 4 cups

Vegetarian with a vegan option

1 cup olive oil, plus more as needed

2 or 3 garlic cloves, thinly sliced

2 shallots, thinly sliced

1 heaping teaspoon fresh thyme leaves, plus several sprigs for the jars

2 bay leaves

1 1/2 teaspoons kosher salt, plus more as needed

1 pound hedgehog or assorted mushrooms, halved or quartered (6 to 8 cups)

3 or 4 oil-packed sun-dried tomatoes, drained and finely chopped

3 tablespoons sherry vinegar

3 tablespoons white wine vinegar

2 teaspoons honey or agave nectar

1/2 cup water

Freshly ground black pepper

**OPTIONAL ADDITIONS**

Fresh lemon juice

Chopped fresh mild herbs, such as parsley, basil, or tarragon

A dish as simple as this calls for good quality ingredients. Use fruity, extra-virgin olive oil, an aged sherry vinegar, and dense, button-type mushrooms. Hedgehogs are the perfect choice, though other meaty mushrooms will work well too. Think buttons, cremini, chanterelles, lobster, or porcini mushrooms and a mixture makes it even more interesting. Chop all the mushrooms into bite-size pieces and clean any foraged or soiled mushrooms with a quick water rinse just before cooking. Make the conserva a day ahead of when you want to serve it and bring to room temperature or gently warm before serving.

Conserva is a perfect addition to an antipasto platter or served alongside roasted meats or chicken. Top grilled bread slices spread with whipped chèvre (see page 102) with the conserva for an easy first course, and pair with warm greens or salad for a quick, light meal. The mushrooms will keep for weeks in the refrigerator if you can resist the urge to snack on them.

Heat the oil in a large, deep saucepan with a lid over medium-low heat. Add the garlic, shallots, thyme leaves, bay leaves, and salt and sauté for 3 to 4 minutes, or until the shallots are translucent and the garlic is beginning to turn golden. Stir in the mushrooms and tomatoes, cover the pan, and cook, stirring often, for 8 to 10 minutes, or until the mushrooms have softened and given up their liquid. (They will release a good amount of liquid.)

Add the sherry vinegar, wine vinegar, honey, and water, increase the heat to medium-high, and bring to a boil. Cook, stirring, for about 2 minutes. Remove the pan from the heat and let cool. Taste, and adjust the seasoning with salt and pepper to taste.

*continued »*

Ladle the mixture into jars or a large, sealable glass container and add 1 or 2 thyme sprigs to each jar. The mushrooms should be completely covered with liquid. Top with more oil or water if necessary. At this point you can transfer the jars to a water bath and process for canning, or store in the refrigerator for 3 to 4 weeks.

For a little extra zest, add a squeeze of fresh lemon juice and a sprinkle of chopped fresh herbs before serving.

# WHIPPED CHÈVRE WITH FRESH HERBS

Makes about 1 1/2 cups

Vegetarian

6 ounces goat cheese, at room temperature

4 ounces cream cheese, at room temperature

1 tablespoon olive oil, plus more for serving

1 teaspoon fresh lemon juice

1 teaspoon honey, plus more for serving

1 tablespoon minced fresh herbs, such as parsley, thyme, or basil

Kosher salt

Freshly ground black pepper

Spread this simple, light, and creamy cheese on a warm piece of grilled sourdough then spoon on a helping of the Wild Mushroom Conserva. Save any leftover to top a burger, mix into a creamy pasta dish, or add to scrambled eggs. Will keep for 3 to 4 days in an airtight container in the refrigerator.

Combine the goat cheese, cream cheese, olive oil, lemon juice, and honey in a food processor or blender and pulse until smooth. Alternatively, whisk together in a bowl by hand. Stir in the fresh herbs. Taste, and season with salt and pepper. Top with an extra drizzle of olive oil or honey before serving.

# CREAM OF CORN AND HEDGEHOG SOUP WITH SAGE AND PINE NUTS

Serves 4

Vegetarian

3 tablespoons butter or ghee

1 large shallot, finely chopped

2 garlic cloves, thinly sliced

8 ounces hedgehog mushrooms, sliced (about 3 cups)

1 teaspoon kosher salt, plus more as needed

1 cup fresh or thawed frozen corn

1 teaspoon dried sage

Pinch of ground nutmeg

3 tablespoons dry sherry, plus more for serving

3 cups Mushroom Broth (page 231), vegetable stock, or chicken stock, plus more as needed

$1/2$ cup heavy cream

Freshly ground black pepper

Toasted and lightly salted pine nuts, for serving

Fried sage leaves (see Note), for serving

Hedgehog mushrooms shine in this silky and savory mushroom soup, wonderful for chilly fall days. Fresh corn and cream bring a luxurious sweetness to the soup, and toasted pine nuts add a bit of salty crunch and accentuate the nutty flavor of the mushrooms. The soup is rich, so a small bowl should satisfy most guests. If you prefer a heartier texture, reserve about one-third of the sautéed mushrooms before blending the soup and stir them in before serving.

In a medium soup pot or deep saucepan over medium heat, melt the butter. Add the shallot and garlic and cook for 2 to 3 minutes, or until softened. Add the mushrooms and salt and sauté for 8 to 10 minutes, or until the mushrooms are lightly colored, cooked through, and tender. (At this point you may want to reserve some of the mushrooms as a garnish for the finished soup.) Stir in the corn, sage, nutmeg, and sherry and continue sautéing for an additional 1 to 2 minutes. Lower the heat, pour in the broth, stir, and gently simmer for 8 to 10 minutes, or until the vegetables are softened.

Let cool for a few minutes. Transfer the soup to a blender or food processor and blend until smooth. Pour the purée back into the pan, stir in the cream, and simmer over medium-low heat, thinning with a little additional stock if needed, for 5 to 6 minutes.

Taste, and adjust the seasoning with salt and pepper. Ladle into bowls, top with a sprinkle of toasted pine nuts, fried sage, and reserved mushrooms (if using). Add a drizzle of sherry and enjoy!

**NOTE:** To fry leafy herbs such as sage leaves, pour a scant $1/2$ inch of a neutral oil into a deep skillet over medium heat. When the oil begins to shimmer, sprinkle in the herbs. Using tongs or a slotted spoon, remove the herbs from the skillet when they begin to crisp and have just turned bright green, 5 to 10 seconds. Don't let them brown. Drain on paper towels and lightly salt.

HUITLACOCHE

*Ustilago maydis*

**PERFECTLY FORMED** rows of corn kernels usually thrive in well-maintained, sunny cornfields. But to farmers' despair, during the annual rainy seasons, the maize may evolve overnight into almost unrecognizable, grayish knobs. The fungus can render an ear unsaleable, but to the delight of Mexican corn farmers, from that blight emerges a prized delicacy of Mexico—huitlacoche!

Huitlacoche, often referred to as "corn smut," is now being sold commercially, so it has been given more appealing names like "corn mushrooms" or "corn truffles." It is popularly used in fillings for tacos or quesadillas, blended into soups, or in sauces for grilled meats and chicken.

## NUTRITIONAL VALUE

The fungus improves the nutritional content of the corn. Huitlacoche is rich in magnesium, calcium, and sodium. It has elevated levels of lysine and cholesterol-reducing beta-glucans.

## SELECTION AND STORAGE

Fresh huitlacoche is available in the late summer through winter. You may find it in specialty markets during the season. If you find it fresh, it can be frozen directly on a baking sheet and stored in ziplock freezer bags.

## COOKING METHODS

Pan-fry, purée, sauté, add to soups

## COOKING TIPS

The flavor is earthy, similar to morels, with the nuttiness of truffles and a wonderful, sweet smokiness from the corn's sugars. "It may have been ambrosia of the Aztec gods, with an inky, mushroomy flavor that is almost impossible to describe," wrote Diana Kennedy, author of *The Cuisines of Mexico*.

Fresh huitlacoche is delicious in flavor and texture. Consider yourself lucky if you find it! If not, you may find it frozen, which is an excellent and the best alternative since it's usually available year-round. When cooked, the corn has a pleasantly soft and slightly chewy texture and is healthier than regular corn, with higher levels of protein and lysine. A third option, although lacking in flavor, is canned huitlacoche, which is packed in citric acid. Still, it's a fair substitute to use in tacos or quesadillas and it's generally available online or from your local Mexican grocer.

## FLAVOR PAIRINGS

- Avocado
- Beef
- Cheese
- Chicken
- Chiles
- Chili powder
- Chorizo
- Cilantro
- Eggs
- Garlic
- Lobster
- Mexican cuisine
- Onions
- Peppers
- Scallops
- Shrimp
- Tomatoes

# HUITLACOCHE QUESADILLA WITH MAITAKE AND ROASTED CHIPOTLE SALSA

Serves 4 to 6

Vegetarian

**ROASTED CHIPOTLE SALSA**

I small onion, peeled and quartered

1 large or 2 small jalapeño peppers

2 garlic cloves, peeled

3 plum tomatoes or 2 medium tomatoes

2 canned chipotle chiles in adobo sauce

1/3 cup fresh cilantro leaves

2 tablespoons fresh lime juice, plus more as needed

Pinch of granulated sugar

Kosher salt

Street vendors throughout Mexico City sell likely the most popular preparation of huitlacoche: quesadillas. In these quesadillas, rich gooey cheese and earthy maitakes perfectly complement the corn mushrooms. A bonus—this recipe works just fine with canned huitlacoche. Pair the quesadilla with Roasted Chipotle Salsa, a smoky salsa you'll also want to spoon on tacos, grilled fish or chicken, eggs, or simply enjoy with a big bowl of tortilla chips.

---

Preheat the oven to 425 degrees F.

**TO MAKE THE SALSA,** place the onion, jalapeño, garlic, and tomatoes on a baking sheet and roast for 15 to 20 minutes, or until the vegetables are lightly charred.

Transfer the vegetables to a food processor or blender, add the chipotle chiles, cilantro, and lime juice, and blend until almost smooth.

## QUESADILLAS

2 tablespoons grapeseed oil or
butter, plus more as needed

1 medium onion, diced

2 garlic cloves, minced

2 jalapeño or serrano peppers,
stemmed, seeded, and
chopped

Pinch of kosher salt, plus more
as needed

4 ounces maitake or other
earthy mushrooms, trimmed
and roughly chopped (about
2 cups)

2 plum tomatoes, diced

1 cup huitlacoche, fresh, frozen,
or canned

1 teaspoon dried epazote or
cilantro

Freshly ground black pepper

8 (6-inch) blue, white, or yellow
corn tortillas

2 cups shredded Mexican
melting cheese, ideally
asadero or Chihuahua

Transfer to a bowl. Taste, and adjust the seasoning with lime juice, sugar, and salt to taste. Cover and store any unused salsa in the refrigerator for up to 1 week.

**TO MAKE THE QUESADILLAS,** heat the oil in a large saucepan over medium-low heat. Add the onion, garlic, jalapeños, and salt and sauté for 4 to 5 minutes, or until just softened. Transfer the onion mixture to a plate and raise the heat to medium-high, adding more oil if needed. Place the maitake mushrooms in the pan, stir, and sauté for 7 to 8 minutes, stirring occasionally, until cooked through and golden and crispy. Add the tomatoes, huitlacoche, and epazote and cook, stirring often for 5 to 6 minutes, or until the mixture has thickened and come together. Add a splash of water if the filling becomes too dry. Adjust the seasoning with salt and pepper. Remove the pan from heat.

Place a large skillet over medium-high heat. Lightly oil the tortillas and, working in batches as needed, spread onto the skillet. Top with a portion of the filling and shredded cheese. Using a spatula, fold the tortillas in half. Press the tortillas down in the skillet and cook for about 1 minute, or until crispy and lightly browned. Carefully flip over the tortillas and crisp the other side. The filling should be hot and the cheese nice and melty. Serve with Roasted Chipotle Salsa.

# BLACK BEAN AND HUITLACOCHE SOUP

¼ cup canola or vegetable oil,
or lard if available

½ medium onion, chopped

3 garlic cloves, thinly sliced

3 cups cooked black beans,
drained if canned

2 cups homemade chicken
stock, plus more as needed

1 teaspoon dried oregano or
½ teaspoon dried Mexican
oregano

1 teaspoon ancho chile powder

½ teaspoon ground cumin

1 tablespoon adobo sauce

½ cup fresh or frozen
huitlacoche

Kosher salt

Freshly ground black pepper

**OPTIONAL TOPPINGS**

Crema

Avocado slices

Sliced fresh chiles

Toasted pepitas

Chopped fresh cilantro

Tortilla strips

Earthy black beans and huitlacoche simmer in a rich, chili-flavored stock, resulting in a richly dark, smoky, and slightly spicy, soup.

Heat the oil in a medium skillet over medium heat. Add the onion and garlic and sauté for 2 to 3 minutes, or until softened. Add the beans, stock, oregano, ancho chile powder, cumin, adobo sauce, and huitlacoche and cook, stirring often, for 15 to 20 minutes.

Transfer the mixture to a blender and purée. Pour the soup back into the pot and continue to cook, adding more stock to reach your preferred consistency, for a few more minutes, or until heated through. Taste, and adjust the seasoning with salt and pepper. Garnish with any of the optional toppings and serve.

# PORCINI-CRUSTED PORK CHOPS WITH HUITLACOCHE SAUCE

**PICKLED ONIONS**

1 medium red onion, thinly
sliced

1/2 cup apple cider vinegar or
white wine vinegar

2 tablespoons granulated sugar

1 teaspoon kosher salt

1 or 2 bay leaves

4 or 5 peppercorns

1 teaspoon dried oregano

1/2 cup water

**HUITLACOCHE SAUCE**

2 small dried pasilla or ancho
chiles

1 cup hot water, plus more as
needed

2 tablespoons butter

1/2 onion, chopped

1 garlic clove, sliced

1 1/2 cups fresh or frozen
huitlacoche

1 cup veal stock, chicken stock,
or vegetable stock

1 teaspoon dried epazote or
cilantro

2 tablespoons heavy cream

Kosher salt

Huitlacoche sauce with a wonderful smokiness on its own, is flavored with fruity, dried pasilla peppers, adding another layer of complexity to the sauce. A perfect match for pan-seared, porcini-crusted pork chops. The pickled onions bring brightness and an extra pop of flavor. Any extra sauce can be used on tacos, burritos, roasted meats, sandwiches, and even eggs. If using canned huitlacoche, which is somewhat salty, wait to adjust the seasoning until after the mixture is cooked and puréed. Porcini powder is available in the spice sections of most grocery stores.

---

**TO MAKE THE PICKLED ONIONS,** place the onion slices in a glass or metal bowl. In a saucepan over medium heat, combine the vinegar, sugar, salt, bay leaves, peppercorns, oregano, and water and cook, stirring occasionally, until the sugar and salt are dissolved. Pour the mixture over the onions, cover, and refrigerate for at least 2 hours and up to 3 weeks.

**TO MAKE THE HUITLACOCHE SAUCE,** remove the stems and seeds from the chiles and place in a medium skillet over medium-high heat. Quickly sear the chiles for about 1 1/2 minutes per side—the color will deepen and the chiles will begin to curl. Immediately transfer to a bowl with enough hot water to cover the chiles, and soak for about 20 minutes, or until softened. Strain, reserving the chiles and 1/2 cup of the soaking liquid (see Rehydrating Dried Chile Peppers, opposite).

Melt the butter in a saucepan over medium-low heat. Add the onion and garlic and sauté for 2 to 3 minutes, or until softened. Stir in the huitlacoche, the chiles and reserved soaking water, stock, and epazote and simmer, partially covered, for 15 to 20 minutes. Let cool.

Transfer the mixture to a food processor or blender and purée. Return the mixture to the saucepan and stir in the cream. Simmer for 2 to 3 minutes, or until the sauce has thickened slightly and is heated through. Taste, and adjust the seasoning with salt, if needed.

## PORCINI-CRUSTED PORK CHOPS

1 tablespoon porcini powder

¼ teaspoon garlic powder

½ teaspoon smoked paprika

2 teaspoons coarse salt

½ teaspoon freshly ground
   black pepper

4 medium, bone-in pork chops

2 tablespoons leaf lard, ghee, or
   vegetable oil

### OPTIONAL TOPPINGS

Crema

Cotija cheese

Fresh cilantro

Fresh corn

**TO MAKE THE PORK CHOPS,** in a small bowl, thoroughly mix the porcini powder, garlic powder, paprika, salt, and pepper.

Lightly coat the pork chops with the porcini powder mixture. Add the lard to an extra-large, heavy skillet over medium-high heat. When the lard is melted and hot, sear the pork chops for about 4 minutes per side, or until cooked to your preference. Remove from the heat.

**TO SERVE,** place the pork chops on individual plates and generously drizzle with the huitlacoche sauce. Top with the pickled onions and any of the optional toppings.

## REHYDRATING DRIED CHILE PEPPERS

Dried chiles are easy to find in most grocery stores. Look for ones that are still soft, older chiles tend to be dry and brittle.

Wipe the chiles first with a damp towel, then cut off the stems and cut them lengthwise. Remove the seeds and veins and tear the chiles into large pieces. Using a spatula, press the chile pieces into the bottom of a hot skillet for about 1½ minutes per side. Remove the pan from the heat, add enough hot water to cover, and set them aside to soak for 20 to 30 minutes, or until softened. The chiles are now ready to blend into your sauce. Taste the soaking liquid, if it's not bitter, use it in the sauce or replace it with stock.

# KING TRUMPET
*Pleurotus eryngii*

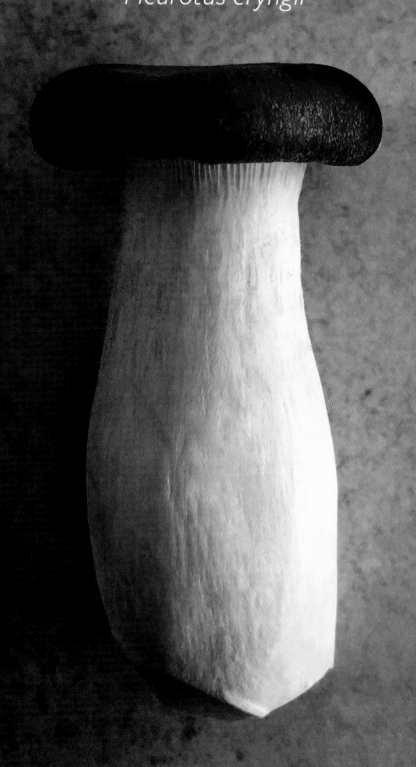

ONE OF the most popular cultivated mushrooms, the king trumpet, grows wild in Southern Europe and North Africa. However, its popularity as a fine-eating mushroom has mostly grown from its prolific cultivation in Asia, Italy, and now too, the United States.

Although considered in the same family as other oyster mushrooms, king trumpet's robust flavor and large, meaty stems set it apart. Usually, 4 to 7 inches in length, their size will vary depending on how they were cultivated. Some of these spectacular mushrooms may weigh up to one pound each!

## NUTRITIONAL VALUE

King trumpets, like all oyster mushrooms, are a significant source of niacin, riboflavin, pantothenic acid, and vitamin D. Their consumption supports healthy cholesterol levels and reduces fat accumulation in the liver.

## SELECTION AND STORAGE

Wrinkling in the caps or stems means they are past their prime. The stems should be creamy white with few spots or blemishes.

Trumpets have a long shelf life and keep well in the refrigerator wrapped in paper towels and placed in a paper bag. Stored properly they should stay in good shape for one week to 10 days.

## COOKING METHODS

Grill, roast, sauté, stir-fry

## COOKING TIPS

King trumpets have a mild flavor when raw, and cooking brings out their deep, umami flavor. The stems are meaty and sometimes tough. For a more tender result, marinate them and/or cut them into slices before cooking. A popular preparation is to cut the stems of the larger varieties crosswise into scallop-like rounds and sear them in butter. They make a surprisingly good stand-in for seafood scallops!

King trumpets are also good for the grill. Cut them lengthwise into $1/3$- to $1/2$-inch-thick pieces, soak them in your favorite marinade, and grill them for a great side dish or pair them with steak.

## FLAVOR PAIRINGS

- Barbecue sauce
- Butter
- Cream
- Eggs
- Garlic
- Hoisin
- Lemon
- Miso
- Olive oil
- Pasta
- Rice, long grain
- Soy sauce
- Spinach
- Tarragon
- Thyme

# KING TRUMPET BÁHN MÌ

Serves 2

Vegetarian

## PICKLED VEGETABLES

¼ cup rice vinegar

1 tablespoon granulated sugar

Pinch of kosher salt

½ cup (2-inch) julienned carrot

⅓ cup (2-inch) julienned daikon
   radish

## MARINADE

1 tablespoon hoisin sauce

1½ teaspoons soy sauce

1½ teaspoons rice vinegar

½ teaspoon granulated sugar

1 small garlic clove, grated

1 tablespoon grapeseed or
   canola oil

4 ounces large king trumpet
   mushrooms (about 2 mushrooms), cut lengthwise into
   ¼-inch slices

2 (6-inch) Vietnamese or French
   baguettes

⅓ cup Shiitake Pâté (page 214)

⅓ cup mayonnaise (preferably
   Japanese Kewpie)

## OPTIONAL TOPPINGS

Chopped fresh cilantro

Sliced cucumber

Sliced chiles

Grilled king trumpets add a smoky umami flavor and meaty texture to this vegetarian but otherwise traditional-style Báhn Mì sandwich. If you can't find trumpets, use black pearl oyster mushrooms or slice large portobello mushrooms.

Blanching large king trumpet mushrooms will make them more tender; if you are using oyster or portobello mushrooms then skip this step.

TO MAKE THE PICKLED VEGETABLES, in a medium glass bowl, combine the vinegar, sugar, and salt and stir until the sugar is dissolved. Add the carrot and daikon and marinate for at least 1 hour or overnight. The pickles can be made up to 3 days in advance.

TO MAKE THE MARINADE, in a medium bowl, whisk together the hoisin sauce, soy sauce, vinegar, sugar, garlic, and oil; set aside. Bring a medium pot of water to a boil over high heat. Add the trumpet slices and blanch for 2 to 3 minutes. Drain the mushrooms, add them to the marinade, and marinate, covered, at room temperature for at least 30 minutes or refrigerated for up to 4 hours.

TO GRILL THE MUSHROOMS, heat a grill or a grill pan to medium-high heat. Remove the mushrooms from the marinade, drain, and grill for 2 to 3 minutes per side, or until the mushrooms are fully cooked and grill marks appear.

TO SERVE, drain the vegetables from the pickling liquid. Cut the baguettes in half lengthwise. Spread the pâté on 1 cut side of each of the baguettes. Spread a generous amount of the mayonnaise on top of the pâté. (Spread both on both sides of the baguette if you're feeling indulgent!) Layer 2 of the baguette halves with half of the mushrooms, then add the pickled carrots and daikon, and cilantro, cucumber, and chiles (if using). Close with the tops and serve.

# KING TRUMPET CHAR SIU

Serves 2 to 3 as an appetizer

Vegetarian with a vegan option

1 small garlic clove, grated

1/2 cup hoisin sauce

2 tablespoons low-sodium soy sauce

1 1/2 tablespoons red bean curd paste

1/2 teaspoon Chinese five-spice powder

2 tablespoons honey or agave syrup

1 teaspoon fresh lime juice

1/2 teaspoon toasted sesame oil

2 tablespoons Shaoxing wine or mirin

2 or 3 drops red food coloring (optional)

1 tablespoon grapeseed or canola oil

2 tablespoons water

12 ounces king trumpet mushrooms (3 or 4) cut lengthwise into 1/3-inch-thick slices

2 or 3 green onions, green parts only, thinly sliced

Cooked white rice, for serving

King trumpet mushrooms are a stand-in for pork in this flavorful Chinese barbecue recipe.

Char siu is a Cantonese-style barbecue, made with a colorful sauce, sweet from hoisin and honey, flavored with five-spice powder, and blended with a key ingredient, bean curd paste. Made from red bean curd with added spices, you'll find the paste online or in most Asian markets. If you like the true red color of traditional char siu, add a few drops of red food coloring. Taste and adjust the honey and seasoning in this sauce; not all hoisin sauces are the same.

Save any leftover sauce in a lidded jar in the refrigerator for a couple of weeks. It's fantastic on pork or chicken.

---

In a medium bowl, whisk together the garlic, hoisin sauce, soy sauce, bean curd paste, five-spice powder, honey, lime juice, sesame oil, wine, red food coloring (if using), oil, and water. Add the mushrooms and toss thoroughly to coat. Marinate for 30 minutes or up to 4 hours in the refrigerator.

Preheat a grill or grill pan to high heat. Drain the mushrooms, reserving the marinade. Grill the mushrooms, basting with the marinade occasionally, for 2 to 3 minutes per side, or until grill marks appear.

Garnish with green onions and serve over white rice.

# BLACK GARLIC BBQ KING
# TRUMPETS WITH SPICY SOBA

Serves 4

Vegan

**MARINADE**

1/2 cup hoisin sauce

1/4 cup dry sherry

1/4 cup soy sauce

1/4 cup granulated sugar

2 tablespoons grated peeled
  fresh ginger

2/3 cup ketchup

1/4 cup seasoned rice vinegar

2 garlic cloves, minced

2 black garlic cloves, crushed into
  a paste with a fork

1/4 teaspoon Chinese five-spice
  powder

2 green onions, minced

2 teaspoons toasted sesame oil

1 pound king trumpet mushrooms
  (5 to 7), sliced lengthwise into
  1/3-inch-thick slices

**SPICY SOBA**

2/3 cup water

2 teaspoons sesame oil

1/4 teaspoon chili oil

Pinch of kosher salt

7 ounces soba noodles

**TO SERVE**

2 tablespoons chopped fresh
  herbs, such as cilantro, mint,
  or basil

Toasted sesame seeds

**OPTIONAL TOPPINGS**

Mung bean sprouts

Peanuts

Red bell pepper, very thinly sliced

The grilling marinade for this recipe has been graciously shared by award-winning barbecue chef, Ray Sheehan, whose sensational sauces have been voted the best in the world. He's also a well-respected barbecue judge, the author of two award-winning cookbooks, and a good friend. The marinade is wonderful on trumpets, but just wait until you try it on chicken or pork!

---

**TO MAKE THE MARINADE,** in a medium saucepan, combine the hoisin sauce, sherry, soy sauce, sugar, ginger, ketchup, vinegar, garlic, black garlic, five-spice powder, green onions, and sesame oil and simmer over medium-low heat for 8 to 10 minutes, or until the sauce has slightly thickened. Add the mushrooms and gently toss to coat. Marinate for at least 30 minutes or up to 8 hours in the refrigerator. Drain the mushrooms, reserving 1/4 cup of the marinade and transfer to a plate.

**TO MAKE THE SOBA,** in a small saucepan over medium-low heat, combine the reserved marinade and water. Add the sesame oil, chili oil, and salt and bring to a simmer. Cook at a low simmer until the sauce has reduced to a glaze, 4 to 5 minutes (you should have about 2/3 cup). Cover, remove from the heat, and keep warm.

Bring a large pot of water to a boil over high heat. Add the soba noodles and cook according to the package instructions. Drain and toss in a large bowl with half (about 1/3 cup) of the sauce; set the remaining sauce aside.

**TO GRILL THE MUSHROOMS,** preheat a grill or a grill pan to medium heat.

Place the mushrooms on the grill and cook, turning once, for 2 to 3 minutes, or until cooked through and grill marks have appeared.

**TO SERVE,** divide the mushrooms over the soba noodles, pour the remaining sauce over the top, and garnish with the herbs and sesame seeds. If you like, top with the bean sprouts, peanuts, and sliced bell peppers for an extra boost of crunchy texture and flavor.

# LION'S MANE
## *Hericium erinaceus*

UNIQUELY BEAUTIFUL, snowball-like formations of shaggy lion's mane grow naturally on the logs and trunks of dead hardwoods in Europe, North America, and Asia. In the U.S., you'll find lion's mane growing in late summer and fall in the southern parts of the country. They grow in clusters with solid middles and stems, and soft, ivory spines on the exterior. They're a safe mushroom for beginner foragers since there are no poisonous look-alikes. Lion's mane mushrooms are often available in many grocery stores and farmers' markets, and easily purchased online.

Lion's mane is an easy mushroom to cultivate, and can be grown indoors from fruiting kits. Powders and tinctures are available at health stores or online promoting its many health benefits.

## NUTRITIONAL VALUE

Lion's mane has a long history of use in East Asian medicine, particularly in China and Japan. Traditionally the mushroom was used for stomach ailments and digestive issues. Today lion's mane is most famous for its incredible brain-boosting benefits and has been used to treat cognitive impairment. It has the ability to stabilize blood serotonin and dopamine levels, and early research shows promise in treating Parkinson's and Alzheimer's diseases.

Lion's mane contains potassium, zinc, iron, germanium, selenium, phosphorus, and all essential amino acids, as well as polysaccharides and polypeptides.

## SELECTION AND STORAGE

If you're fortunate enough to find a cluster while foraging, be careful when trimming the mushroom away from its base. If you leave a little of the stem, you can look forward to finding more growing from the same spot at the same location, year after year.

Lion's mane stores well. Wrapped in paper towels in a partially open plastic storage bag and stored in the refrigerator, it should last for at least a week or more. Be sure to change the paper towels if they've become damp. And if the edges of the mushrooms turn dark yellow or light brown, carefully trim them away—the interior will still be fresh and edible. Discard any mushrooms that become slimy or moldy.

For longer term storing, freezing is a good option. Because of their high water content, it is best to cook them first. A quick blanch or sauté will do; then cool completely and store in freezer bags, removing as much excess air as possible. You don't need to thaw before cooking. The mushrooms can also be dried for even longer-term storage.

## COOKING METHODS

Bake, fry, roast, sauté

## COOKING TIPS

The flavor of these mushrooms is mild with a subtle seafood flavor once they've been cooked. With their shreddable consistency, they are a terrific substitute for crab and, overall, they make a good seafood replacement in vegan recipes.

To prepare them, tear the mushrooms into bite-size pieces and sauté them in butter with a little water or stock for 20 to 30 minutes, or until tender. You can then add them to crab cakes, Asian dumplings, creamy soups, pasta dishes, or use for topping crostini, etc. Or cut them into slices, sauté in butter, and finish the dish with a light sauce.

## FLAVOR PAIRINGS

- Basil
- Bell peppers: red, yellow
- Breadcrumbs
- Butter
- Cream
- Cream cheese
- Curry
- Lemon
- Mayonnaise
- Pasta
- Soups
- Soy
- Tarragon
- Tomatoes
- Wine, white

# LION'S MANE RANGOON

3 tablespoons butter

1 small garlic clove, minced

4 ounces cleaned, shredded, and chopped lion's mane mushrooms (about 2 cups)

4 tablespoons water, divided

$\frac{1}{2}$ teaspoon salt, plus more as needed

1 cup whipped cream cheese

1 green onion, green part only, finely chopped

$\frac{1}{2}$ teaspoon Worcestershire sauce

$\frac{1}{2}$ teaspoon fresh lemon juice

Freshly ground black pepper

1 egg

24 wonton wrappers

Peanut or vegetable oil, for frying

Sweet chili sauce or sweet and sour sauce, for serving

A delicious mushroom version of the ever-popular Crab Rangoon, this is a super-easy make-ahead party appetizer.

Melt the butter in a medium saucepan over medium-low heat. Add the garlic and sauté for 2 to 3 minutes, or until just golden. Stir in the mushrooms, 2 tablespoons of water, and the salt and cook, stirring occasionally, for 10 to 12 minutes, or until the mushrooms are tender and the water has been absorbed. Set aside to cool.

In a medium bowl, combine the cream cheese, green onion, Worcestershire sauce, and lemon juice and mix well. Fold in the mushrooms. Taste, and adjust the seasoning with salt and pepper. (The mixture can be covered and refrigerated at this point for several hours or overnight.)

In a small bowl, whisk together the egg and the remaining 2 tablespoons of water.

Place a heaping teaspoon of the mushroom mixture in the center of a wonton wrapper. Brush the edges with the egg wash and fold it into a triangle shape, sealing the edges. Repeat with the rest of the wrappers and filling. Alternatively, place the filling in the center of each wonton wrapper, brush the edges with egg wash, and then pinch up and seal the edges like a little purse.

Heat 2 to 3 inches of oil in a large, heavy saucepan to 330 to 350 degrees F. Add the wontons, a few at a time, and fry, gently turning, until golden brown, about 2 minutes. Drain the wontons on a wire rack or on paper towels, and repeat until all of the wontons are cooked. Move them to a baking sheet and keep warm in a low oven until ready to serve.

Serve with sweet chili sauce or sweet and sour sauce.

# CRISPY LION'S MANE FRIED "FISH" SANDWICH

Serves 4

Vegetarian

5 to 6 ounces medium to large lion's mane mushrooms (3 or 4 mushrooms)

2 cups buttermilk

$^1/_2$ cup all-purpose flour

1 tablespoon Old Bay seasoning

Grated zest of $^1/_2$ lemon

1 teaspoon kosher salt, plus more as needed

2 eggs

2 tablespoons water

2 cups finely crushed panko breadcrumbs

Peanut or vegetable oil, for frying

4 slices American cheese (optional)

4 soft sandwich buns

Shredded lettuce, for serving

This delicious fried lion's mane sandwich doesn't stray far from your classic, favorite fast-food fish sandwich. Buttermilk-marinated lion's mane is fried until crispy and served on a soft bun with a slice of American cheese, lettuce, and with a healthy dollop of tangy tartar sauce.

Fresh lion's mane should be tender and sweet with a minimal amount of "grassy" flavor. Some of the larger sections (called for in this recipe), can be a little tough or stringy. A quick soak in buttermilk tenderizes and smooths the flavor (see page 87). Keep the oil no hotter than 350 degrees F. If the oil is too hot the exterior will overcook, and the mushrooms may be underdone.

Slice the mushrooms, from top to stem into $^1/_3$- to $^1/_2$-inch-thick cutlets. Trim any tough stem pieces and lightly score any tough stem parts crosswise. Marinate in the buttermilk for 1 hour or overnight in the refrigerator.

In a medium bowl, thoroughly mix the flour with the Old Bay seasoning, lemon zest, and salt. In a shallow bowl, whisk the eggs with the water, and place the panko into a third bowl.

Remove the mushrooms from the buttermilk, and using your hands, gently but firmly squeeze out the excess moisture until almost dry. Form into 4 patty shapes, coat with the seasoned flour, dip into the egg wash, and thoroughly coat with the breadcrumbs, pressing lightly to adhere to the mushrooms and slightly compress the patties. Transfer to a plate.

Heat $^1/_2$ inch of oil in a large, heavy skillet or saucepan over medium-high heat. When the oil begins to shimmer and is 350 degrees F, lower the breaded mushrooms into the hot oil and fry for 2 to 3 minutes per side, or until golden brown and crispy (4 to 6 minutes total). Transfer to paper towels to drain, and lightly sprinkle with salt. Add a slice of cheese if using.

## TARTAR SAUCE

1 cup mayonnaise

2 tablespoons buttermilk

1 tablespoon minced shallot

3 tablespoons sweet pickle relish

2 teaspoons Dijon mustard

2 tablespoons fresh lemon juice

Kosher salt

Freshly ground black pepper

## OPTIONAL TOPPINGS

Sliced tomatoes

Pickles

Sliced red onion

**TO MAKE THE TARTAR SAUCE,** in a small bowl, mix the mayonnaise, buttermilk, shallot, relish, mustard, and lemon juice and season with salt and pepper. Leftover tartar sauce will last for a week, refrigerated.

**TO SERVE,** generously spread the tartar sauce on the bottom and top halves of the buns. Add the lion's mane cutlets, lettuce, and any optional toppings to the bottom buns, and then add the bun tops.

**NOTE:** For a snack or appetizer, make crispy nuggets! Trim the stems and cut the mushrooms into 2-inch pieces, follow the recipe through frying, and serve with your favorite dipping sauce.

# LION'S MANE BOLOGNESE

2 tablespoons olive oil, divided

1 tablespoon butter

$1/2$ onion, finely chopped

$1/2$ teaspoon kosher salt, plus more as needed

$1/2$ fennel bulb, finely chopped

1 small carrot, finely chopped

3 garlic cloves, minced

Pinch of red pepper flakes

8 ounces lion's mane mushrooms, finely chopped (about $3^{1}/2$ cups)

2 tablespoons double-concentrated tomato paste

$1/2$ cup dry white wine

14 ounces (about 2 cups) passata or San Marzano tomato sauce

1 cup roasted vegetable stock or chicken stock, divided

1 cup whole milk or cream, divided

1 Parmesan rind

Freshly ground black pepper

12 ounces dried spaghetti or another long pasta

$1/4$ cup grated Parmesan cheese, plus more for serving

A flavor-rich bolognese is usually well worth the time it takes to prepare. Luckily, this mushroom bolognese takes less time than the traditional meat version, but still, it's absolutely necessary to patiently allow the layers of flavor to develop slowly by caramelizing the vegetables at each step. And don't forget the Parmesan rind!

Heat 1 tablespoon of the olive oil and the butter in a large saucepan over medium heat. Add the onion, a pinch of salt, and cook for 2 to 3 minutes, or until translucent. Add the fennel, carrot, and a pinch of salt and sauté for 10 to 12 minutes, or until the vegetables are softened and caramelized. Stir in the garlic and pepper flakes and cook for an additional minute.

Add the remaining 1 tablespoon of olive oil to the pan, stir in the mushrooms, $1/2$ teaspoon of salt, and cook, until the mushrooms turn golden brown, 5 to 6 minutes. Add the tomato paste and cook, stirring often, for 3 to 4 minutes, or until the mixture is thickened and the paste has lost its bright color. Stir in the wine and cook until it reduces by half. Add the passata, $1/2$ cup of stock, and $1/2$ cup of the milk and stir until combined. Add the Parmesan rind and cook at a low simmer, for 45 to 60 minutes, adding a little more stock and milk as the mixture cooks down, until the flavors have developed and the sauce has thickened. Remove the Parmesan rind, and then taste and adjust the seasoning with salt and pepper.

Bring a large pot of salted water to a boil over high heat. Add the pasta and cook for 7 to 10 minutes, or until al dente. Drain the pasta, reserving $1/2$ cup of the pasta water. Add the pasta to the pan with the sauce and toss to combine. Add a little of the pasta water and continue to toss and cook—the pasta sauce should cling nicely to the pasta. Add the grated Parmesan cheese and toss thoroughly. Serve with additional Parmesan cheese.

# LOBSTER MUSHROOM

*Hypomyces lactifluorum*

# LOBSTER MUSHROOMS

**LOBSTER MUSHROOMS** are the tasty result of a parasitic mold that overtakes Russula and Lactarius mushrooms, transforming their ho-hum persona into large, shell-shaped, strikingly red brackets with an irresistible scent of steamy lobster. These mushrooms are found from mid-July through October, mainly in New England and in the northern areas of the West Coast.

## NUTRITIONAL VALUE

Lobster mushrooms are an excellent source of fiber and vitamins D and A, B complex, and vitamin C, which helps boost and support the immune system. They also contain significant amounts of copper, iron, calcium, and moderate amounts of protein.

## SELECTION AND STORAGE

Look for mushrooms that have a heavy feel. Older mushrooms are lighter in weight. Pick those with bright coloring and avoid harvesting or purchasing any lobster mushrooms that have mold or are deep purple or brown. Consume them within a few days after harvesting and do not keep them longer than a couple of days after cooking. Eating older lobster mushrooms that appear purple or brown and may be contaminated with bacteria or mold can make you ill.

Store young lobster mushrooms in a kitchen dishcloth or brown paper bag in the refrigerator for up to a week. They also freeze well. Clean, trim and, if necessary, cut them into pieces, place them on trays in a single layer, and freeze until solid. Store in airtight freezer bags or containers.

Drying lobster mushrooms really brings out their lobster essence. If you plan on using lobster mushrooms in a dish, save a few to dry and make into a quick stock to enhance their mild, seafood-like flavor.

## COOKING METHODS

Braise, fry, sauté, and add to soups and sauces

## COOKING TIPS

Light to yellow sections of these mushrooms are tender with a nutty flavor. The deeper red parts of the mushrooms have a slightly seafood-like taste with a dense texture. A quick blanch in boiling water before cooking will help soften these more mature sections of the mushrooms.

Although named lobster mushroom, the taste is only slightly reminiscent of seafood. The intensified lobster aroma from reconstituting dried mushrooms in hot water makes them perfect for vegan stocks and soups when you want a hint of seafood flavor. They will also add a tint of red-orange color.

As with all mushrooms that are new to you—especially foraged—proceed with caution and sample small amounts before indulging in larger quantities.

## FLAVOR PAIRINGS

- Brandy
- Butter
- Celery
- Cream
- Lemon
- Onion
- Parsley
- Pasta
- Rice, risotto
- Soups
- Stocks
- Tarragon
- Tomato
- Wine, dry white

# LOBSTER MUSHROOM VOL-AU-VENT

Serves 2

Vegetarian

1/4 ounce dried lobster mushrooms (3 or 4 pieces)

1 cup water plus 1 tablespoon water, divided

1 sheet frozen puff pastry, thawed

1 egg

2 tablespoons butter, divided

1 small leek, white and light green parts only, halved, cleaned, and thinly sliced

1 garlic clove, minced

4 ounces fresh lobster mushrooms, cleaned and thinly sliced into 1-inch pieces (about 2 cups)

1/2 teaspoon kosher salt, plus more as needed

1 teaspoon brandy

1/3 cup heavy cream

1 tarragon sprig

Freshly ground black pepper

Handful fresh parsley leaves, or julienned basil leaves, for garnish

A classic, and slightly decadent starter, the lobster mushrooms step in for the seafood. The rounds are large enough to make a satisfying first course or a lunch indulgence paired with a small salad. This recipe doubles easily for more servings.

In a small saucepan over medium heat, combine the dried mushrooms and 1 cup of water and bring to a simmer. Turn off the heat, cover, and steep for 20 to 25 minutes, or until softened. Strain and chop the mushrooms and reserve the liquid (stock).

Roll out the puff pastry and cut it into 4 (4-inch) rounds. Cut 2 of the rounds with a 2-inch cutter, to create 2 (4-inch) rings and 2 (2-inch) rounds. In a small bowl, whisk together the egg and 1 tablespoon of water to create an egg wash. Brush the edges of the 2 (4-inch) rounds and place a 4-inch ring on each. Place the rounds on a nonstick baking sheet and brush the tops with the egg wash. Refrigerate while the oven is heating.

Preheat the oven to 425 degrees F.

Bake the rounds for 12 to 14 minutes, or until the pastries are golden and puffed. Remove from the oven and let cool.

Heat 1 tablespoon of the butter in a large saucepan over medium-low heat. Add the leek and sauté for about 2 minutes, or until just tender. Add the garlic and cook for an additional minute. Add the remaining 1 tablespoon of butter, both fresh and rehydrated dried mushrooms, and salt and cook for 6 to 8 minutes, or until the mushrooms turn golden. Add the brandy, 1/2 cup of the reserved stock, cream, and tarragon sprig, bring to a simmer, and cook, stirring often and adding more stock, if necessary, for 8 to 10 minutes, or until the mushrooms are softened and the mixture is lush and creamy. Remove the tarragon sprig and season with additional salt and pepper.

Spoon the mixture over the puff pastry cups, garnish with fresh parsley, and serve.

# LOBSTER MUSHROOM RISOTTO

Serves 4

Vegetarian

3 tablespoons butter or ghee, divided

1/2 cup panko breadcrumbs

Pinch of kosher salt, plus more as needed

4 cups Lobster Mushroom Stock (page 234) or store-bought lobster or seafood stock, plus more as needed

4 ounces lobster mushrooms, trimmed (about 2 cups)

1 shallot, finely chopped

1 cup carnaroli or Arborio rice

1/2 cup white wine

1/4 cup grated Parmesan cheese

2 tablespoons heavy cream or butter

2 tablespoons minced fresh herbs, such as parsley, basil, or tarragon

Grated zest of 1/2 lemon

Freshly ground black pepper

Great stock is key to any good risotto. This lobster mushroom risotto uses a rich, flavorful stock made with dried lobster mushrooms. Cheese is frowned upon with seafood in most Italian dishes, but here the cheese adds a welcome layer of nutty flavor and creaminess.

In a small skillet over medium heat, melt 1 tablespoon of butter. Add the panko and toast, stirring often, for 2 to 3 minutes, or until golden brown and crispy. Lightly season the breadcrumbs with salt and transfer to a plate.

In a medium saucepan over high heat, bring the stock to a boil. Add the mushrooms and blanch for 5 to 6 minutes. Strain the mushrooms, reserving the stock in the saucepan over low heat to keep warm. Cut the mushrooms into thin, bite-size pieces.

Heat the remaining 2 tablespoons of butter in a medium saucepan over medium heat. Add the shallot and sweat for 2 to 3, or until softened. Stir in the mushrooms and sauté for 5 to 6 minutes, until golden and cooked through.

Add the rice and cook, stirring, for 2 to 3 minutes, or until the rice is coated with butter and translucent. Add the wine and cook, stirring, until the wine is absorbed. Add a ladleful of the mushroom stock, and cook, stirring regularly, until the stock is absorbed. Continue adding stock, a ladleful at a time, cooking and stirring, for a total of about 25 minutes, or until the rice is tender. The risotto should be creamy; if it is too loose, cook a bit longer, if it's too thick, add more stock.

To finish, vigorously stir in the Parmesan cheese and heavy cream. Fold in the fresh herbs and lemon zest. Taste, and adjust the seasoning with salt and pepper. Add a generous sprinkle of toasted breadcrumbs and serve.

# LOBSTER MUSHROOM FRA DIAVOLO

¹/₄ ounce dried lobster mushrooms

2 cups water

4 tablespoons butter, divided

8 ounces fresh lobster mushrooms, cleaned and cut into ¹/₂-inch pieces (about 4 cups)

1 teaspoon kosher salt, divided, plus more as needed

2 shallots, finely chopped

¹/₂ cup finely chopped fennel

4 garlic cloves, minced

2 tablespoons double-concentrated tomato paste

¹/₂ cup white wine

1 (28-ounce) can San Marzano plum tomatoes, with juice

¹/₂ to 1 teaspoon red pepper flakes, or 2 Calabrian chiles minced, plus more as needed

Pinch of granulated sugar (optional)

1 tablespoon brandy

Freshly ground black pepper

1 pound spaghetti, linguine, or fettuccine

2 tablespoons chopped fresh parsley leaves

Fra diavolo is a beloved, spicy Italian tomato sauce usually made with shrimp or lobster and served over linguine or other long pasta. Roughly translating to "among the devil," the red pepper flakes give it the signature heat. In this vegetarian version, lobster mushrooms take the place of seafood.

Use San Marzano tomatoes if you can find them, and a really good high quality olive oil.

---

In a medium saucepan over medium heat, combine the dried mushrooms and water and bring to a simmer. Turn the heat to medium-low and simmer for 30 to 45 minutes, or until the liquid has reduced by almost half. Strain and reserve the liquid. Chop the mushrooms and set aside.

Heat 3 tablespoons of the butter in a large, deep skillet over medium heat. Add the fresh lobster mushrooms and ¹/₂ teaspoon of salt and sauté for 5 to 6 minutes, or until golden. Transfer the mushrooms to a plate.

Add the shallots, fennel, garlic, and pinch of salt, stir, and sauté for 3 to 4 minutes, or until the vegetables are softened. Stir in the reserved dried and fresh mushrooms, add the tomato paste, and cook, stirring, until the paste has darkened in color. Add the wine and reduce by half. Add the tomatoes, pepper flakes, and the remaining ¹/₂ teaspoon of salt. Pour in the reserved lobster mushroom liquid and cook, partially covered, breaking up the tomatoes and stirring occasionally, for 25 to 30 minutes. (Add a pinch of sugar if the tomatoes are tart.) Stir in the brandy and the remaining 1 tablespoon of butter and cook, uncovered, for a few minutes longer, or until the flavors have developed and the sauce has thickened a bit. Taste and adjust the seasoning with salt and pepper. Cover and remove from the heat.

Bring a large pot of lightly salted water to a boil over high heat. Add the pasta and cook for 8 to 10 minutes, or until al dente. Drain, reserving 1 cup of the pasta water.

Place the pan with the sauce back over medium heat, add the pasta, and toss with the sauce. Add some of the reserved pasta water, a little at a time, stirring and tossing until the sauce has coated the pasta. Serve in pasta bowls and garnish with the parsley.

# MAITAKE
## *Grifola frondosa*

NATIVE TO AREAS of Japan, China, and North America, maitake are found growing at the foot of oak, elm, and maple trees. Their striking, mottled brown appearance resembles a cluster of chickens, earning their nickname, "hen of the woods." In Japan, according to folklore, Buddhist nuns discovered maitake fruiting under trees. The nuns were so excited that they erupted into a dancing celebration, earning the maitake another name, "dancing mushroom." These highly valued mushrooms grow in temperate areas from late summer through November. Luckily, they are easy to cultivate and available for purchase year-round.

## NUTRITIONAL VALUE

Maitake not only have physical beauty and superb culinary qualities, they have also been used in traditional Chinese and Japanese medicine for thousands of years as a medicinal mushroom. Considered an adaptogenic mushroom, they are believed to help the body adapt to stress.

Maitake are a rich source of niacin, a reasonably good source of folic acid and potassium, have a high vitamin D content, and contain B-complex vitamins, copper, iron, and zinc.

## SELECTION AND STORAGE

Thankfully these mushrooms are now being cultivated and are readily available online and likely at your nearby market. The cultivated ones will not have quite the depth of flavor as those foraged, but they are still an excellent mushroom to enjoy. Look for mushrooms with white stems, without any brown streaks, and a fresh texture—they tend to dry out as they age. Avoid older specimens that are orange or reddish in color; they may be contaminated with bacteria or mold and can make you ill.

Wrap them well in paper towels and place in an open plastic storage bag before refrigerating to keep them in good shape for a week or more. These mushrooms also freeze well. Cut raw mushrooms into steak-size slices, freeze on trays, and store in airtight freezer bags.

They have a high moisture content and do not dry well.

## COOKING METHODS

Braise, fry, grill, roast, sauté

## COOKING TIPS

Maitake mushrooms are versatile and adaptable to a variety of flavors and cooking methods. They have an intensely meaty flavor, and the texture is tender but holds up well to a crispy sear. They readily absorb marinades, roast beautifully, and can be battered and fried. Try cutting them into thick slices, brushing with oil, seasoning with salt and pepper, and finishing on a hot grill. Serve with a lemon-garlic aioli. You won't miss the steak. Shave the tender leaves from the outside and sauté them until crisp to add a savory umami topping to your favorite pasta or potato dish.

## FLAVOR PAIRINGS

- Black garlic
- Butter
- Carrots
- Cheese: Parmesan, provolone
- Eggs
- Fish, salmon
- Garlic
- Ginger
- Lentils
- Miso
- Olive oil
- Oregano
- Polenta
- Prosciutto
- Rice, Arborio
- Rosemary
- Scallions
- Sesame
- Soba
- Sour cream
- Soy
- Spinach
- Thyme
- Vinegar, balsamic
- Walnuts
- Wine: red, Sherry

# MAITAKE PHILLY CHEESESTEAK

**PROVOLONE CHEESE SAUCE**

2 tablespoons butter

2 tablespoons all-purpose flour

1 cup whole milk

3 ounces shredded provolone
cheese

2 ounces grated white American
cheese

Kosher salt

Freshly ground black pepper

Maitake mushrooms have a dense texture and a naturally meaty flavor, making them one of my very favorite mushrooms for a meat substitute. This mushroom makes an authentic-tasting Philly cheesesteak sandwich—it just takes a little well-worth-it-time to caramelize the onions and slow cook the mushrooms in a flavorful jus, finished with a last-minute crisp in the pan. Add more stock at the end if you like a juicy sandwich.

Onions aren't optional, but bell peppers are, so feel free to add them if you like. Hoagie rolls are the top choice for buns. And the cheese? A creamy, gooey provolone—American cheese sauce does the trick. The American cheese keeps the sauce nice and creamy; provolone is classic but substitute cheddar if you prefer. You're going to like this.

**TO MAKE THE SAUCE,** in a medium saucepan over medium-low heat, melt the butter. Add the flour and whisk until the flour and butter are thoroughly combined, and continue to cook for about 2 minutes. Whisk in the milk, bring to a simmer, then stir constantly until the sauce has thickened. Add the cheese, stir until melted, and remove from the heat. Taste and season with salt and pepper.

## MAITAKE CHEESESTEAK

3 tablespoons butter, divided,
plus ¼ cup, at room
temperature

2 tablespoons grapeseed or
other neutral oil, divided, plus
more as needed

1 large sweet onion, halved end
to end and very thinly sliced
lengthwise

Pinch of kosher salt plus
1 teaspoon, divided

1 pound maitake mushrooms,
trimmed and thinly chopped
(about 6 cups)

1½ tablespoons Worcestershire
sauce

1 teaspoon garlic powder

½ teaspoon onion powder

Pinch of granulated sugar

¼ teaspoon freshly ground
black pepper

1½ cups cup low-sodium beef
or roasted vegetable stock

4 (6-inch) hoagie or sandwich
rolls

**TO MAKE THE MAITAKE CHEESESTEAK,** heat 1 tablespoon of the butter and 1 tablespoon of the oil in a large skillet over medium heat. Sauté the onion, with a good pinch of the salt, until softened, deeply caramelized, and golden, about 15 minutes. Transfer the onion to a small bowl.

Preheat the oven to 350 degrees F.

Adjust the heat under the skillet to medium-high. Add the remaining 2 tablespoons of butter and 1 tablespoon of oil, and working in batches, sauté the mushrooms, adding more oil if necessary, until they are cooked through and nicely browned.

Add the cooked onions back into the skillet. Add the Worcestershire sauce, garlic and onion powders, sugar, 1 teaspoon of salt, and the pepper and stir. Add ½ cup of the stock and cook until the liquid is absorbed. Stir in another ½ cup of stock, cover, and turn the heat to low. Cook for an additional 8 to 10 minutes, or until the mushrooms are softened, then uncover and turn the heat to medium-high to crisp the mushrooms lightly. (Add some of the remaining stock if you prefer an extra juicy sandwich.) Stir and remove from the heat.

**TO SERVE,** split the hoagie rolls, leaving one side intact. Spread the room-temperature butter on the cut sides of the rolls, place on a baking sheet, and toast in the oven until lightly browned, 3 to 4 minutes. Remove from the oven and spoon a generous helping of the cheese sauce on the bottom halves of the buns. Place a quarter of the mushroom mixture on top of each sandwich and drizzle with another spoonful of cheese sauce. Bring out plenty of napkins and enjoy!

# RISOTTO ALLA MILANESE WITH ROASTED MAITAKE

1 1/2 tablespoons balsamic
   vinegar
2 tablespoons white miso paste
2 teaspoons low-sodium soy
   sauce
1 garlic clove, grated
1/4 cup grapeseed oil or
   vegetable oil
8 ounces maitake mushrooms,
   cut or torn into 1/2- to 1-inch
   pieces (about 4 cups)
Pinch of kosher salt, plus more
   as needed
4 cups chicken stock,
   Mushroom Broth (page
   231), or vegetable stock,
   plus more as needed
3 tablespoons butter, divided
1 shallot, minced
1/2 fennel bulb, trimmed and cut
   into small dice (about 1/2 cup)
1 1/2 cups Arborio rice
Pinch of saffron threads,
   crumbled
1/2 cup white wine
Freshly ground black pepper
1/2 cup grated Parmesan cheese,
   plus more, for serving

Maitake mushrooms are lightly marinated in balsamic vinegar and miso, and roasted until tender yet crisp. Combined with caramelized fennel and a hint of saffron they make a mouth-watering risotto. This is spectacular paired with duck.

Preheat the oven to 425 degrees F. Place a wire rack in a baking sheet.

In a small bowl, whisk together the vinegar, miso paste, soy sauce, garlic, and oil. Brush or lightly coat the mushrooms with the marinade and sprinkle with the salt. Place the mushrooms on the prepared baking sheet and roast for 12 to 14 minutes, or until lightly browned and crispy. Cool, and chop the mushrooms into bite-size pieces, cover loosely with aluminum foil, and set aside.

In a medium saucepan over medium heat, bring the stock to a low simmer, turn the heat to low, cover, and keep warm.

In a large skillet over medium-low heat, melt 2 tablespoons of the butter. Add the shallot and fennel and sauté for 5 to 6 minutes, or until softened. Raise the heat to medium-high, add the rice, stir, and cook for 2 to 3 minutes, or until translucent. Add the saffron threads and toast in the saucepan for 1 to 2 minutes. Add the wine, stir, and continue to cook and stir until the wine is absorbed. Add the stock, 1 ladleful at time, stirring constantly, and adding more stock as each ladleful is absorbed. After about 15 minutes of cooking, stir in the reserved maitakes, and continue to cook, adding stock as needed, for a total of 25 to 30 minutes, or until the rice is tender.

The risotto should be nice and creamy, if the risotto seems dry, add more stock. Taste, adjust the seasoning with salt and pepper, add the remaining 1 tablespoon of butter, and the Parmesan cheese. Stir briskly to thoroughly combine and serve immediately with additional grated Parmesan.

# GRILLED MAITAKE AND BITTER LETTUCE SALAD WITH HONEY-GLAZED WALNUTS AND GOAT CHEESE

Serves 4

Vegetarian

2 tablespoons red wine vinegar

1 teaspoon Dijon mustard

1 teaspoon fresh lemon juice

½ small garlic clove, grated

½ cup walnut oil

Kosher salt

Freshly ground black pepper

1 tablespoon butter

2 tablespoons honey

1 cup walnut halves or pieces

8 ounces maitake mushrooms, cut into 4 to 6 (⅓-inch-thick) slices

Olive oil, for brushing

1 small head radicchio, torn or chopped

2 cups torn or chopped endive, romaine, or leaf lettuce

Crumbled goat cheese, for serving

This is light dinner or lunch salad that you'll want to make again and again. Uncork a nice Pinot Grigio and enjoy!

In a small bowl, vigorously whisk together the vinegar, mustard, lemon juice, garlic, and walnut oil. Taste, and season with salt and pepper. Set aside.

In a small sauté pan over medium heat, melt the butter. Add the honey and walnuts and cook, stirring often, for about 5 minutes, or until the walnuts are glazed and lightly toasted. Spread out on a plate to cool. (You'll have a few leftover for snacking!)

Preheat a grill or a grill pan to medium heat.

Brush the maitake slices with olive oil and season with salt and pepper. Grill the mushrooms for about 2 minutes per side, or until grill marks appear. Transfer to a plate.

Arrange the lettuces on individual plates. Top each with the grilled maitake. Drizzle with the walnut vinaigrette and top with the candied walnuts and crumbled goat cheese.

# MARINATED MAITAKE "STEAKS"

2 teaspoons soy sauce

1 teaspoon Worcestershire sauce

½ garlic clove, grated

½ teaspoon dried oregano

¼ teaspoon kosher salt, plus more as needed

⅛ teaspoon freshly ground black pepper, plus more as needed

¼ cup olive oil, or more if you prefer a less intense marinade

6 ounces maitake mushrooms (3 or 4), cut into ⅓- to ½-inch-thick slices

You don't need a long soak in this marinade, just a few minutes will do. Try it with other types of mushrooms; portobellos and oysters are also good choices. This recipe makes enough for two servings, simply double or triple the recipe for more.

In a medium bowl, whisk together the soy sauce, Worcestershire sauce, garlic, oregano, salt, pepper, and olive oil. Add the maitake mushrooms and marinate for up to 30 minutes. Alternatively, brush the marinade on the mushrooms a few minutes before grilling.

Preheat a grill or a grill pan to medium-high heat.

Grill the mushrooms, turning once, for 2 to 3 minutes, or until cooked through and grill marks have appeared. Season with additional salt and pepper to taste.

# MATSUTAKE
## *Tricholoma matsutake*

THE HIGHLY ESTEEMED and extraordinary matsutake has long been revered in Asia, particularly Japan, for its unique and intense flavor and as a symbol of happiness and fertility. They are as beloved in Japan as the truffle is in France, being difficult to find, adored, and very, very, expensive.

Also known as "pine mushrooms," the word "matsu" equals pine and "take" refers to mushroom in Japanese.

Matsutake are mycorrhizal and form symbiotic relationships with the roots of trees, especially favoring pines. Found in East and Southeast Asia, talented foragers in North America may spot them in California and the Pacific Northwest from September through January.

## NUTRITIONAL VALUE

Matsutake mushrooms are a good source of B vitamins, protein, copper, potassium, zinc, and selenium. One hundred grams of matsutake contains at least 200 percent of the recommended daily allowance of vitamin D and vitamin B3, 49 percent of potassium, and 100 percent of copper.

## SELECTION AND STORAGE

Choose smaller, younger mushrooms, ideally with unbroken veils and intact caps. The fresher looking, the better. Wipe them with a damp cloth or paper towel before cooking or storing them, rather than cleaning with water.

They will store well wrapped in paper towels in an unsealed plastic bag. Their aroma will fade quickly, so use or preserve them within a day or two. The ideal method for preserving matsutake is by freezing. Freeze raw matsutakes on a sheet pan until solid. Wrap each mushroom in aluminum foil, place them in an airtight freezer bag, and freeze for up to three months. Partially thaw them for easy slicing before cooking.

Drying does change and lessen the flavor somewhat, but it still is a satisfactory way to preserve matsutake for up to a year.

## COOKING METHODS

Cook in rice or broth, fry, grill, sauté

## COOKING TIPS

Unsurprisingly, the matsutake's symbiotic relationships with pine trees give them an intense piney, woodsy flavor, which is somewhat spicy with a hint of cinnamon. The flavor is a bit pungent and that can be off-putting to some people. Taste and use sparingly at first.

The Japanese enjoy matsutake cooked with rice or broth in a well-known aromatic rice dish referred to as Matsutake Gohan. The mushrooms are simply cooked in Japanese rice and dashi, to showcase the mushroom's unique flavor and aroma.

Some believe matsutake clash with dairy; however, I find them sublime when cooked in a butter sauce with Japanese wine. They pair beautifully with sablefish (black cod) and are delicious on the grill or fried in crispy tempura and served with a tangy dipping sauce.

## FLAVOR PAIRINGS

- Butter
- Cabbage
- Chervil
- Chicken
- Chives
- Cream
- Dashi

- Fish: cod, sablefish
- Garlic
- Ginger
- Lemon
- Olive oil
- Parsley

- Rice
- Scallions
- Sesame oil
- Shallots
- Shrimp
- Soy
- Tarragon

- Tempura
- Vinegar, rice
- Wine: Japanese, mirin, sake

# MATSUTAKE GIN FIZZ

2 ounces Matsutake-Infused Gin
  (recipe follows)
1 tablespoon fresh lemon juice
1 tablespoon simple syrup
1 egg white
Ice
2 ounces club soda
Lemon or orange twist, for
  garnish

Gin pairs beautifully with pine-scented matsutake mushrooms—no surprise, these mycorrhizal mushrooms grow near the base of stately pine trees. Enjoy the steeped gin straight with just a splash of club soda or use it in any gin cocktail that gives the matsutake center stage.

In a cocktail shaker, combine the infused gin, lemon juice, simple syrup, and egg white and shake for 15 seconds. Fill the shaker with ice and continue shaking for another 30 seconds until cold. Strain the mixture into a glass and top with the club soda. The egg white will form a foam on top of the cocktail.

Rim and garnish with a lemon twist and serve immediately.

# MATSUTAKE-INFUSED GIN

2 grams dried matsutake
  (2 or 3 pieces)
1 (1 1/2 × 1-inch) piece orange
  peel
8 ounces gin

In a small, sealable glass jar or bottle, combine the matsutake, orange peel, and gin. Steep for 12 to 24 hours or to taste. Store unused infused gin in the refrigerator for up to 3 months.

# MATSUTAKE TEMPURA WITH YUZU-LEMONGRASS AIOLI

8 ounces matsutake mushrooms

½ cup good quality mayonnaise (preferably Japanese Kewpie)

1 tablespoon yuzu juice

2 teaspoons lemongrass paste

1 garlic clove, minced

Pinch of kosher salt

1 cup cake flour

1 large egg

1 cup cold club soda or water

Peanut or canola oil, for frying

2 tablespoons sesame oil

Coarse salt

Fresh Thai basil leaves, for garnish (optional)

Matsutake mushrooms are fried in a light, crispy tempura batter and paired with a tangy, citrusy, yuzu-lemongrass aioli in this recipe. Lemongrass paste has additional spices and is a flavorful alternative to fresh lemongrass. You'll find it at most grocery stores.

Tempura is all about cold! Cold club soda or water slows the development of the gluten, resulting in light, crispy tempura. If you're new to deep-frying, you might want to experiment with a piece of onion or another vegetable until you feel comfortable using your precious matsutakes. With a little practice, you'll have it down in no time. Expand the recipe with additional tempura-inspired ingredients if you like. Shrimp, asparagus, bell pepper rings, onions, sweet potatoes, and squash are all good choices.

---

Place a medium bowl in the refrigerator to chill for at least 20 minutes while preparing the matsutake and aioli. Trim and cut the matsutake into ¼- to ⅓-inch slices and set aside. Line a plate with paper towels.

In a small bowl, whisk together the mayonnaise, yuzu juice, lemongrass paste, garlic, and kosher salt. Set aside.

Remove the chilled bowl from the refrigerator. Combine the flour, egg, and club soda in the bowl and stir. Don't overmix, a few lumps are okay. Place the bowl with the batter in the refrigerator until you're ready to cook.

Fill a large heavy pot with 1 1/2 to 2 inches of peanut oil, add the sesame oil, and bring it to 325 degrees F over medium-high heat.

When the oil reaches the correct temperature, remove the bowl of tempura batter from the refrigerator. Using a spider spinner, and working with a few pieces at a time, dip the mushroom slices into the batter, add them to the pot, and fry for 1 to 2 minutes, or until golden. Transfer the mushrooms to the paper towel–lined plate to drain. Sprinkle with coarse salt. Scoop out the crunchy, flavorful deep-fried bits floating in the oil and add them to the plate with the cooked matsutake. Add the Thai basil leaves (if using) to the oil and fry for a few seconds. Transfer to the paper towel–lined plate.

Serve the tempura garnished with the fried basil and the aioli alongside for dipping.

**NOTE:** Strain and store used oil in a container with a lid, such as an empty sauce bottle.

# MATSUTAKE RISOTTO

Serves 4

Vegetarian

7 or 8 grams dried matsutake mushrooms (⅓ cup)

1 tablespoon low-sodium soy sauce

1 teaspoon kosher salt, plus more as needed

5 cups water

5 tablespoons butter, divided, plus more as needed

¾ cup finely chopped fresh matsutake mushrooms (3 or 4 medium), plus 1 matsutake, cut into 4 to 6 slices

1 shallot, minced

1 cup carnaroli or Arborio rice

⅓ cup sake or Shaoxing wine

Fresh lemon juice, for seasoning

Freshly ground black pepper

Fresh chives, chopped, for garnish

Rice and matsutake are a beloved and classic combination, especially in Japanese cuisine. Use a light dashi instead of matsutake stock if you are unable to source dried matsutake mushrooms.

In a large pot over medium-high heat, bring the dried mushrooms, soy sauce, salt, and water to a boil. Cover, turn off the heat, and steep for about 20 minutes. Remove the mushrooms, finely chop, and set aside. Place the pot with the stock back on the stove over medium-low heat, keeping it just below a simmer.

Heat 2 tablespoons of butter in a risotto pan or a large saucepan over medium-high heat. When the butter foams, add the finely chopped fresh matsutake and the reserved rehydrated matsutake, and sauté, adding a pinch of salt midway through the cooking, for 4 to 5 minutes, or until golden and crispy. Transfer the mushrooms to a plate. Add the sliced mushroom to the saucepan, adding more butter if needed, and cook for 2 to 4 minutes, or until golden. Lightly season with salt, set aside on a separate plate, and keep warm.

Heat 2 tablespoons of butter in a large heavy saucepan over medium-low heat. Add the shallot and sauté for 2 to 3 minutes, or until just softened. Add the rice and cook, stirring often, for 2 to 3 minutes, or until the rice is coated with butter and translucent, and gives off a nutty aroma. Raise the heat to medium-high, add the sake and cook, stirring until the sake is absorbed. Add 1 ladleful of the reserved stock and cook, stirring until the liquid is absorbed. Continue to add the stock, cook, and stir, for 20 to 25 minutes, or until each ladleful is absorbed and the rice is tender but slightly firm to the bite. Stir in the reserved mushrooms and briefly cook to reheat them. Add the remaining 1 tablespoon of butter and a squeeze of lemon juice and stir well. Adjust the seasoning with salt and pepper as needed.

Serve immediately garnished with the reserved mushroom slices and chives.

# MISO-GLAZED BLACK COD WITH MATSUTAKE AND SAKE-LEMON BUTTER

**MISO-GLAZED BLACK COD**

2 tablespoons white miso paste

2 teaspoons brown sugar

1/2 teaspoon sesame oil

2 tablespoons butter

2 to 3 tablespoons grapeseed oil or another neutral oil

4 (4- to 6-ounce) pieces black cod, with or without the skin

Cooked rice or vermicelli, for serving (optional)

**MATSUTAKE AND SAKE-LEMON BUTTER**

2 tablespoons grapeseed oil, other neutral oil, or ghee (do not use plain butter as oil gives the skin a wonderful crisp)

4 ounces matsutake mushrooms, thinly sliced (about 2 cups)

3 tablespoons sake

3 tablespoons mirin

1 tablespoon fresh lemon juice

6 tablespoons chilled butter

Kosher salt

Ground white pepper

2 tablespoons chopped fresh herbs, such as tarragon, parsley, or chives

Elegantly light, this recipe using black cod pairs beautifully with matsutake. Fresh black cod is a fish you'll remember once you've tried it. It's delicate and sweet, and a perfect backdrop for the matsutake mushrooms. The cod is lightly coated with a sweet miso glaze and the lemony butter sauce finishes the dish with a nice hit of citrus. Serve over rice or vermicelli.

**TO MAKE THE GLAZED COD,** in a small saucepan over low heat, combine the miso paste, brown sugar, sesame oil, and butter and whisk until smooth. Remove from the heat.

Heat the oil in a nonstick skillet over medium-high heat. Pat the cod dry with a paper towel. When the oil is hot, add the cod, skin side down, and sear (leaving the cod undisturbed) for about 4 minutes, or until the skin is crisp and the fish is mostly cooked. Brush the tops with the miso glaze. Turn over the cod and cook for an additional minute, or until lightly golden. (If the cod is skinless, sear for 3 to 4 minutes, or until the fish is two-thirds cooked through before turning over.) Transfer the cod to a plate and keep warm.

**TO MAKE THE MATSUTAKE AND SAKE-LEMON BUTTER,** wipe out the skillet, place it back on the stovetop over medium-high, add the grapeseed oil, and sauté the matsutake for 4 to 5 minutes, or until lightly golden and crispy. Remove from the skillet.

Lower the heat to medium, add the sake, mirin, and lemon juice and bring to a simmer. Remove the skillet from the heat and whisk in the chilled butter, 1 tablespoon at a time. Taste, and adjust the seasoning with salt and pepper. Gently stir in the cooked matsutake.

**TO SERVE,** place the cod on individual plates (over rice or vermicelli if using), and spoon the matsutake mushrooms and lemon-butter sauce over the top. Sprinkle with fresh herbs and serve.

# MOREL
*Morchella deliciosa*

# MORELS are one of the most highly prized mushrooms in the world! They come in at least

four different colors, characterized as black, olive, yellow, and gray. So far over 19 varieties have been discovered, with more likely to be found in the future. Morels grow in fertile, organic soil and when fully mature, they reach up to six inches in height. Typically foraged during the spring, they are often found in abundance around the base of elm, ash, aspen, cottonwood, and oak trees.

## NUTRITIONAL VALUE

Morels are high in protein and fiber and, along with chanterelles, contain more vitamin D than almost any other mushroom. They also contain generous amounts of iron, copper, manganese, zinc, niacin, and vitamins E and $B_6$. They are loaded with antioxidants, and help repair liver damage and balance blood sugar.

## SELECTION AND STORAGE

Morels do need some care when storing since they tend to dry out quickly. They keep fairly well in the refrigerator, thoroughly wrapped in paper towels and placed in an unsealed plastic storage bag—a method that helps retain moisture.

For ideal long-term storage, dry your morels. They are one of the very best mushrooms for drying because they retain their flavor and shape after rehydrating in stock or water.

Alternatively, you can sauté and freeze morels on baking sheets and store in airtight containers before freezing them for months-long storage.

## COOKING METHODS

Add, chopped, to soups and sauces, braise, fry, roast, sauté, stuff

## COOKING TIPS

One of the most desirable mushrooms you may come across, morels are an eagerly awaited culinary treat when they arrive in the springtime. They have a robust, earthy flavor and a meaty texture with a distinctive honeycomb-like shape. Perfectly hollow inside, they offer a tasty vessel for stuffing and are equally delicious when braised or quickly sautéed in butter with a splash of cream to finish. Pair them with other long-awaited spring delicacies like fresh peas and young onions.

Foraged morels trap sand and grit in their pits and will likely need cleaning; soak them in cold salted water for a bit, then drain and pat dry before cooking.

Morels should never be eaten raw to avoid a nasty stomach upset.

## FLAVOR PAIRINGS

- Asian cuisine
- Bacon
- Broth
- Butter
- Cheese: Asiago, fontina, Parmesan
- Chicken
- Crab
- Cream
- Duck
- Eggs
- Fennel
- Garlic
- Parsley
- Pork
- Shrimp
- Tarragon

# MOREL MINI QUICHE

Serves 6

Vegetarian

1 sheet pie dough, thawed if frozen

1 tablespoon butter

$2/3$ cup diced fresh morel mushrooms or other fresh mushrooms, such as cremini, button, or oyster, stemmed and diced

$1/2$ teaspoon kosher salt, plus more as needed

Freshly ground black pepper

6 large eggs

$1/3$ cup heavy cream

$1/2$ cup whole milk

$1 1/4$ cups finely grated Gruyère cheese

Pinch of granulated sugar

Pinch of freshly grated nutmeg

2 tablespoons finely chopped fresh herbs, such as parsley, tarragon, chives, or a mixture

Morels make a surprise appearance in these French-inspired mini quiches. The recipe closely resembles the little egg tarts you'll find in bakeries all over France. Gruyère is wonderful with morels, but Swiss or even fontina is a good stand-in. Feel free to make your own variations using different mushrooms and cheeses, and add ham or pancetta, bacon, leeks, etc. Use a standard 6-cup muffin pan, a $9 1/2$-inch tart pan, a $9 1/2$-inch quiche or pie pan, or a mini-muffin pan for two-bite appetizers.

Freezing the pie dough in the muffin pan(s) before baking creates a super-flaky crust. Use your favorite pie dough recipe, Cynthia's Pie Crust (page 179), or a good store-bought pie dough works just fine as a quick substitute. Be careful not to overbake, as the tarts will continue to cook after you remove them from the oven. The quiches can be made ahead, frozen, and briefly reheated for an easy light dinner or brunch for guests.

Coat or spray a 6-cup muffin pan with oil. On a clean work surface, roll out the pie dough to an 8 × 12-inch sheet. Using a $3 1/2$- to 4-inch circular pastry cutter, cut the dough into 6 rounds. Press a circle of dough into each muffin cup. Place in the freezer until ready to bake.

Preheat the oven to 400 degrees F.

Heat the butter in a skillet over medium-high heat. Add the mushrooms and sauté for 4 to 5 minutes, or until lightly golden and cooked through. Taste, and season with salt and pepper and transfer to a plate to cool.

In a medium bowl, whisk together the eggs, cream, milk, cheese, sugar, nutmeg, and $1/2$ teaspoon of salt. Stir in the cooled mushrooms and fresh herbs.

Spoon the egg mixture into the muffin cups, leaving $1/4$ inch of space from the top. Bake for 20 to 25 minutes, or until the quiches are puffed and golden. Transfer to a wire rack to cool.

# MOREL-PARMESAN CREAM SAUCE

Makes about 1 1/2 cups

Vegetarian

2 tablespoons butter

1 ounce chopped morel mushrooms, fresh or rehydrated
(about 1/2 cup)

1 tablespoon all-purpose flour

1/2 cup Quick Mushroom Broth
(page 230), vegetable
stock, or chicken stock if
using fresh morels, or 1/2 cup
of the soaking liquid from
rehydrated morels

1/2 cup milk

1/2 cup heavy cream

1/4 cup shredded Parmesan
cheese, plus shavings for
garnish

1 tablespoon minced fresh
tarragon

1/2 teaspoon kosher salt

1/4 teaspoon freshly ground
black pepper

This easy, luxurious sauce complements poultry, fish, or vegetables, and it's simply mind-blowing on asparagus.

In a medium saucepan over medium heat, melt the butter and sauté the
morels for 3 to 4 minutes, or until the mushrooms start to give up their
liquid. Stir in the flour and cook for 1 minute. Whisk in the broth or
soaking liquid, add the milk and cream, and bring to a low simmer. Turn
the heat to medium-low and continue to cook for 3 to 4 minutes, or
until the sauce begins to thicken. Stir in the Parmesan cheese and the
tarragon, stir briefly to combine, and add the salt and pepper. Garnish
with the Parmesan shavings.

**NOTE:** Due to their thin exteriors, morels do not readily absorb the
liquid they release during cooking. When you see the liquid, it is an
indicator that they are nearly fully cooked and almost ready to be
removed from the heat.

# MORELS AND PEAS
# WITH RICE SOUBISE

Serves 4

Vegetarian

2 cups salted water (or enough to cover)

½ cup Arborio rice or another short-grained rice

7 tablespoons butter, divided

2 pounds sweet onions, sliced very thinly

Pinch of kosher salt, plus more as needed

¼ teaspoon ground white pepper

½ cup frozen and thawed or fresh peas

¼ cup heavy cream

½ cup grated Gruyère cheese

2 ounces morel mushrooms, cleaned and halved (about 1 cup)

2 tablespoons dry sherry

Freshly ground black pepper

2 tablespoons chopped fresh tarragon leaves or fresh parsley

If you haven't tasted or prepared soubise, an onion-forward cream sauce, I encourage you to try it. Do I really need that many onions, you say? No worries please, the onions melt sweetly into the creamy rice-cheese mixture, and it's absolutely delicious. I've adapted the soubise from Julia Child's recipe in *Mastering the Art of French Cooking*, though in this recipe, I've included earthy sautéed morels plus fresh peas, making this dish a star in its own right, but it makes a great side dish too, with grilled steak or roasts.

Preheat the oven to 300 degrees F.

In a medium saucepan, bring the salted water to a boil over medium-high heat. Add the rice and cook for 5 minutes. Drain immediately and set the rice aside.

In a deep, oven-safe saucepan or Dutch oven with a lid over medium heat, melt 4 tablespoons of the butter. Add the onions in batches, stirring to coat with the butter, and to avoid browning. Stir in the partially cooked rice, salt to taste, and the white pepper.

Cover and bake for 1 hour, stirring once or twice, or until the rice is fully cooked. If not, return the pan to the oven for an additional 10 minutes, or until the rice is tender. Taste, adjust the seasoning with salt, and stir in the peas, cream, and cheese. Keep covered and warm in the oven with the door open and the heat turned off while sautéing the morels.

Heat 1 tablespoon of the butter in a medium saucepan over medium heat. Add the morels and sauté for 4 to 5 minutes, or until cooked through and just beginning to crisp. Add the sherry and cook, tossing the mushrooms, until the liquid is absorbed. Taste, and season with a pinch of salt and pepper to taste. Stir in the remaining 2 tablespoons of butter.

Spoon the soubise into individual dishes, add the sautéed morels, and a drizzle of the pan drippings. Garnish with tarragon leaves or parsley.

# TROFIE WITH MOREL AND WALNUT PESTO

12 ounces trofie or other short,
   dried pasta
1/3 cup Morel and Walnut Pesto
   (opposite)
Kosher salt
Freshly ground black pepper
Grated Parmesan cheese, for
   serving
Walnut oil, for serving

Trofie is a short, thin, twisted pasta from Liguria, Northern
Italy, most often made fresh and paired with pesto. Dried forms
are often available online or in Italian markets. Despite its
smaller size, trofie has a longer cooking time than most pastas.
You can substitute another short, good quality dried pasta like
penne or ziti.

Bring a large pot of salted water to a boil over medium-high heat. Add
the pasta and cook according to the package directions until al dente.
Drain, reserving 1/2 cup of pasta water.

In a deep saucepan over medium heat, combine the pesto with the
pasta and stir well. Add the reserved pasta water, a little at a time, until
the pasta is nicely coated with the sauce (you will likely not need all of
the water). Taste and adjust the seasoning with salt and pepper.

Serve immediately with a little grated cheese and a drizzle of walnut oil.

# MOREL AND WALNUT PESTO

Makes about 1 cup

Vegetarian

2 tablespoons plus ¼ cup
   olive oil
5 ounces morel mushrooms,
   cleaned, stemmed, and
   roughly chopped (about
   3 cups)
½ teaspoon kosher salt, plus
   more as needed
1 large garlic clove, chopped
⅓ cup toasted walnuts
⅓ cup fresh parsley leaves
⅛ cup walnut oil
¼ cup grated Parmesan cheese
1 teaspoon fresh lemon juice
Freshly ground black pepper

A rustic and flavorful pesto made with the ideal pairing of morels and walnuts. Morels often are found growing near the base of walnut trees, another delicious result of Nature's symbiotic pairing.

Heat a large skillet over medium heat. Pour 2 tablespoons of olive oil into the skillet, stir in the mushrooms, sprinkle with the salt and toss. Cook briefly until the mushrooms are cooked through and tender, 6 to 8 minutes. Add the garlic and cook a minute longer, but do not brown the garlic.

Transfer the mushrooms and garlic to the bowl of a food processor and add the walnuts and parsley. Pulse 2 or 3 times until the nuts are minced, and the mixture is well blended. Slowly pour in ¼ cup of olive oil and the walnut oil and process until smooth. Add the Parmesan cheese and lemon juice and process briefly to combine. Taste and adjust the seasoning with salt and pepper.

## MOREL VALUES

I'll share with you a secret,
If you swear not to tell.
About a tasty mushroom,
It's known as the Morel.
Some people plan all winter,
It's why they wait for spring.
To go afield out searching,
For that delightful little thing.

When lilacs have turned purple,
And about to go to bloom,
It's time to be out looking
For your favorite little "schroom."
You'll be putting up with wood ticks,
And nettle weed that stings.
But I guess it's all quite worth it,
For all the joy it brings.

—E. Peter Brunette

# CHICKEN-STUFFED MORELS
# WITH MARSALA SAUCE

## MARSALA SAUCE

2 tablespoons butter

3 shallots, cut lengthwise into
    slices

Pinch of kosher salt, plus more
    as needed

1 1/2 cups Roasted Mushroom
    Stock (page 232), a
    commercial demi-glace,
    or chicken stock

1/3 cup Marsala wine

1 tablespoon cornstarch

1/4 cup water

Freshly ground black pepper

## POLENTA

2 cups water

2 cups whole milk

1 cup quick-cooking (instant)
    polenta

1 teaspoon kosher salt, plus
    more as needed

1/2 cup grated Parmesan cheese

1 tablespoon butter

Freshly ground black pepper

An elegant and easy company dish, the morels can be filled and the sauce made a day ahead. Select the very freshest and larger morels for this impressive main course, clean them well, and trim the stems down to the base. Older morels often are dry and may split and not hold the filling. If you like, substitute duck or pork sausage for the chicken sausage. Use a high quality, full-flavored stock for the sauce, either homemade or store-bought.

Polenta, a common cornmeal porridge popular in Northern Italy, is a perfect accompaniment to the stuffed morels. Traditional polenta takes nearly an hour to cook with constant stirring. (If you have the time, it's the best tasting option.) I included quick-cooking polenta in this recipe, it will cut your cooking time to mere minutes, and with the added milk and Parmesan cheese you'll have a delicious result. Look for a good Italian brand for the best flavor and texture.

---

**TO MAKE THE MARSALA SAUCE,** place a saucepan over medium heat, melt the butter, and sauté the shallots with a pinch of salt for 4 to 5 minutes, or until caramelized. Transfer the shallots to a plate.

Add the stock and Marsala to the saucepan and simmer for 8 to 12 minutes, or until reduced by half. In a small bowl, whisk together the cornstarch and the water. Add the mixture to the saucepan and whisk until smooth. Simmer for an additional 3 to 4 minutes, or until the sauce is thickened. Stir in the cooked shallots, taste, and season with salt and pepper. Cover and keep warm.

**TO MAKE THE POLENTA,** in a deep medium saucepan over high heat, bring the water and milk to a boil. Turn the heat to low, whisk in the polenta and salt, and continue to cook, steadily whisking for 5 to 8 minutes, until thickened and creamy. (Some instant polentas may cook faster, so follow the package directions.) Remove from the heat, stir in the cheese and butter, and adjust the seasoning with additional salt and pepper. Cover and keep warm.

Preheat the oven to 400 degrees F.

## STUFFED MORELS

¼ cup panko breadcrumbs

2 tablespoons milk

6 ounces (about 2 links) raw
  chicken sausage

2 tablespoons minced fresh
  tarragon leaves

¼ cup grated Gruyère cheese

14 to 16 large morel mushrooms, well cleaned and
  stems trimmed

Olive oil, for brushing

Kosher salt

**TO MAKE THE STUFFED MORELS,** in a medium bowl, combine the panko breadcrumbs and milk and let soak for 10 to 15 minutes. Add the sausage, tarragon, and Gruyère cheese, and using a fork, stir until blended. Do not overmix. Using a pastry bag or your fingers, fill the morels with the sausage mixture. (The stuffed morels can be refrigerated at this point for several hours or overnight.) Lightly brush the morels with the olive oil, place on a baking sheet, sprinkle with salt, and roast for 10 to 12 minutes.

**TO SERVE,** spoon the polenta into shallow bowls, add the morels, and drizzle with the Marsala sauce.

**NOTE:** Try serving the stuffed morels by themselves for a quick appetizer with a good mustard sauce for dipping.

# GROWN-UP MOREL "TOTS"

Makes 12 to 15 "tots"

Vegetarian

## LEMON-GARLIC AIOLI

¹⁄₂ cup mayonnaise (preferably Japanese Kewpie)

1¹⁄₂ tablespoons fresh lemon juice

1 garlic clove, grated

¹⁄₂ teaspoon Dijon mustard

2 tablespoons olive oil

Kosher salt

Freshly ground black pepper

Hot sauce, for seasoning (optional)

## MOREL "TOTS"

1 tablespoon butter

2 ounces minced morel mushrooms (about 1 cup)

Pinch of kosher salt, plus more as needed

2 pounds (2 large) russet potatoes, peeled and quartered

1 tablespoon potato starch or cornstarch

²⁄₃ cup grated fontina cheese

2 tablespoons minced fresh chives

Freshly ground black pepper

1 (18-inch) sheet parchment paper, halved lengthwise

Peanut or vegetable oil, for frying

Morels give this recipe an adult spin on a childhood favorite. Simply sautéed and minced morels are mingled with lightly cooked, grated potatoes, mixed with fontina cheese and chives, and then fried to golden crispy perfection. Finely chopped porcini or the "leaves" of maitake would be another great choice in place of morels. Aged cheddar or Gruyère would be a delicious cheese swap. The mixture can be made ahead, formed into logs, and then frozen two to three days ahead of time.

---

**TO MAKE THE AIOLI,** in a medium bowl, combine the mayonnaise, lemon juice, garlic, mustard, and olive oil and whisk vigorously. Taste, and season with salt and pepper, and a dash of hot sauce (if you like a little extra zing). Set aside.

**TO MAKE THE MOREL TOTS,** heat the butter in a medium skillet over medium heat. Add the morels and a pinch of salt, sauté for 3 to 4 minutes, or until the morels are cooked through and are beginning to crisp. Remove from the skillet and set aside.

Bring a medium pot of lightly salted water to a boil over medium-high heat. Add the potatoes and cook for 12 to 15 minutes, or until just barely fork-tender. Drain thoroughly and let cool.

When the potatoes are cool enough to handle, grate them in a food processor or by hand with a box grater. In a medium bowl using a fork, combine the potatoes, morels, potato starch, fontina, and chives. Taste and adjust the seasoning with salt and pepper. Using your hands, gather the potato mixture together and divide it into 2 log shapes. Lay the parchment sheets lengthwise on a work surface. Place each log of potato mixture about 3 inches from the lower long edge and fold the paper over. Roll up the potato mixture and tuck in the sides of the parchment to form into a 1-inch log, about 12 inches long. Twist the ends of the parchment, fold over the edges, and freeze for about 1 hour. (If freezing overnight or longer, allow 20 minutes to thaw before the next step.)

Remove the logs from the freezer and unwrap. Using a sharp knife, cut each log into 1 1/2- to 2-inch "tots." (Alternatively, you can form individual tots by hand.)

Preheat the oven to 350 degrees F.

When you are ready to cook, heat 3 inches of oil in a heavy pot over medium-high heat to about 360 degrees F. If the temperature is too low the tots will stick to the pan. The oil is at the right temperature when it bubbles around a wooden spoon submerged in the oil.

Fry a few tots at a time for 3 to 4 minutes, or until golden and crispy. Transfer the tots to a nonstick baking sheet and bake for 8 to 10 minutes, or until tender. Serve with the aioli.

# NEBRODINI
*Pleurotus nebrodensis*

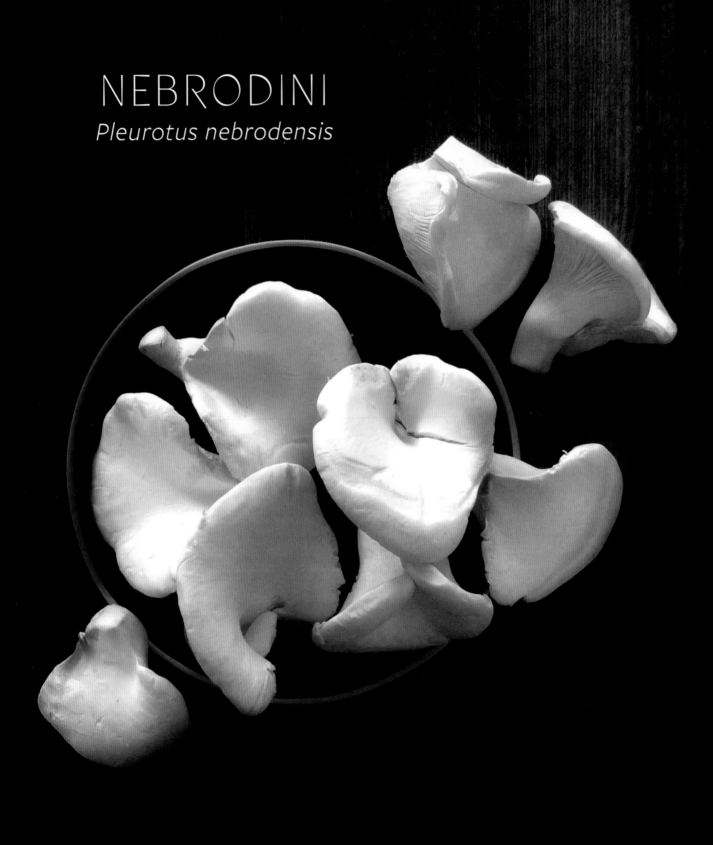

**THE SCULPTURAL** and oh-so-beautiful Nebrodini bianco mushroom grows only on the lush slopes of the Nebrodi mountains of Sicily, where the varied terrain and abundant wildlife provide a dense nutrient ecosystem for over thirty species of mushrooms.

Nebrodini bianco mushrooms, also known in Italy as "Sicilian grilling oysters," are an Italian culinary delicacy cherished locally for their meltingly tender consistency and similarity in flavor to shellfish. Years ago, Sicilian families and chefs roamed the Nebrodi hillsides gathering this much-cherished fungi. Sadly, due to their popularity, overforaging has resulted in near extinction. The mushrooms are now considered critically endangered and harvesting them is illegal.

There is good news: With credit going to British mushroom farmer and cultivator John S. Rowe, Nebrodini are now successfully cultivated in Asia, Europe, Canada, and the United States. Because of John Rowe and a handful of passionate mushroom growers, the cultivated and now plentiful Nebrodini are available to consumers, giving these unique, amazing mushrooms time to re-propagate in their native Sicilian habitat.

## NUTRITIONAL VALUE
Nebrodini mushrooms are a good source of zinc, iron, manganese, calcium, and vitamin D.

## SELECTION AND STORAGE
Look for creamy white mushrooms with few spots; they should be firm and not spongy. Keep them refrigerated, wrapped in paper towels and then inside a paper bag, and they should last for several days.

For long-term storage, freezing is your best option. Sauté them first and add them to your favorite sauce or broth before storing in an airtight container or freezer bag and freezing.

## COOKING METHODS
Fry, grill, sauté, stir-fry

## COOKING TIPS
I absolutely love cooking with these mushrooms; their stunning beauty, flavor, and texture are like no other. They are consistently tender from cap to stem. The taste is mild and slightly sweet, and when sautéed, they develop a delicious flavor reminiscent of fresh calamari or shrimp. This mushroom is delicious as a seafood stand-in for frito misto. They cook beautifully on the grill with a light dressing of olive oil and lemon. Don't resist if you have the chance to buy or taste them.

## FLAVOR PAIRINGS

- Arugula
- Basil
- Broccoli
- Butter
- Capers
- Cheese: Parmesan, ricotta salata
- Chiles, Calabrian
- Fennel
- Garlic
- Leek
- Lemon
- Olive oil
- Pasta
- Tomatoes
- Thyme

# PESTO ALLA TRAPANESE WITH NEBRODINI BIANCO

Serves 4

Vegetarian

**PESTO ALLA TRAPANESE**

4 or 5 ripe plum tomatoes, peeled (see Note) and seeded or 1 (28-ounce) can San Marzano tomatoes, drained and seeds removed

$1/2$ cup blanched almonds, lightly toasted

2 garlic cloves

10 fresh basil leaves, torn

$1/2$ cup grated aged, mild Romano cheese or Parmesan, plus more for serving

$1/4$ cup olive oil

Kosher salt

Freshly ground black pepper

Here is the recipe to make when you have all those ripe summer plum tomatoes from your garden or market. This delicious, tomato-rich pesto is Sicily's answer to Liguria's famous and familiar basil pesto sauce. The Sicilian's take on the sauce uses the same basic ingredients but subs in almonds instead of traditional pine nuts and is finished off the heat to retain the freshness of the herbs and tomatoes.

Traditionally the sauce is prepared with a mortar and pestle, but a food processor does it in a pinch with less effort and excellent results. The classic pasta shape used with this dish is busiate, but gemelli, rigatoni, penne, or cavatappi are all great substitutes.

The sauce pairs beautifully with the nebrodini mushrooms, but you'll likely want to keep this pesto recipe to use all by itself. Broil crusty, Italian bread, layer it with the pesto, and top it with a good melting cheese like fontina or mozzarella. Bake the pesto topped with a round of good goat or sheep's milk cheese for a simple delicious appetizer to spread on crostini. Or toss with roasted vegetables, chicken, or shrimp. The pesto can be kept in the refrigerator in an airtight container for up to one week, or frozen for three to four months.

**TO MAKE THE PESTO,** combine the tomatoes, almonds, garlic, basil, cheese, and olive oil in a mortar and mash with a pestle into a smooth paste. Alternatively, place the ingredients in a food processor and pulse until smooth. Transfer to a bowl and season the pesto with salt and pepper.

### NEBRODINI BIANCO

2 tablespoons olive oil

1 tablespoon butter, plus more
as needed

8 ounces nebrodini bianco
mushrooms, halved and thinly
sliced (3 or 4 large)

1 teaspoon kosher salt

12 ounces pasta, such as
busiate, gemelli, rigatoni,
penne, or cavatappi

**TO MAKE THE NEBRODINI**, heat the olive oil and butter in a large sauce-pan over medium heat until the butter begins to sizzle. Add the mush-rooms in a single layer and sauté for 7 to 8 minutes, or until golden brown on both sides. Add the salt, and remove from the pan.

Bring a large pot of lightly salted water to a boil over medium-high heat. Add the pasta and cook according to the package directions. Drain, reserving 1 cup of the pasta water.

In a large saucepan over low heat, combine the pasta and the pesto and toss until well mixed, adding the reserved pasta water, a little at a time, to make a creamy sauce. Add the mushrooms and toss with the pasta. Top with more cheese if desired and serve.

**NOTE:** To peel the tomatoes, score an X in the tomato skins with a sharp knife and then blanch the fresh tomatoes in simmering water for about 30 seconds. Remove them from the water and peel when they are cool enough to handle.

# GRILLED NEBRODINI BIANCO WITH ARUGULA, PARMESAN, AND THYME

Serves 3 to 4

Vegetarian

## MARINADE

1 tablespoon lemon juice

2 tablespoons extra-virgin olive oil

½ teaspoon kosher salt, plus more as needed

Freshly ground black pepper

8 ounces nebrodini bianco mushrooms, cut into ½-inch slices (about 4 cups)

## LEMON DRESSING

¼ cup fresh lemon juice

2 small garlic cloves, grated

1 teaspoon Dijon mustard

½ teaspoon honey or maple syrup (optional)

1 teaspoon fresh thyme leaves

½ teaspoon sea salt, plus more as needed

⅓ cup extra-virgin olive oil

Kosher salt

Freshly ground black pepper

4 to 5 cups arugula

Shaved or grated Parmesan cheese, for serving

1 cup toasted seasoned breadcrumbs or crumbled, store-bought seasoned croutons

Nebrodini bianco are known as "grilling oysters" in Sicily, and for good reason. They are delicious grilled as a side for roasted chicken or meats, or on top of arugula with a tangy lemon dressing for a refreshing summer salad. Shaved Parmesan and toasted breadcrumbs add a nice finishing texture.

Store leftover lemon dressing in the refrigerator for up to a week—you'll love it on grilled vegetables or chicken.

---

**TO MAKE THE MARINADE,** in a medium bowl, whisk together the lemon juice, olive oil, salt, and pepper. Add the mushrooms and gently toss them with the marinade. Let sit for 10 to 15 minutes.

**TO MAKE THE DRESSING,** in a small bowl, whisk together the lemon juice, garlic, mustard, honey (if using), thyme, salt, and olive oil.

Preheat a grill or grill pan to medium-high heat.

**TO SERVE,** remove the mushrooms from the marinade and place them on the grill at least ½ inch apart and cook for 4 to 5 minutes per side, or until nice grill marks have appeared and the mushrooms are cooked through. Transfer the mushrooms to a plate and season with salt and pepper.

In a large bowl, combine the arugula with the dressing, a little at a time, and toss just until the leaves are well coated. (You will have dressing leftover.) Divide the arugula between individual plates and top with equal portions of the mushrooms. Finish with the Parmesan cheese and the breadcrumbs.

# NEBRODINI BIANCO
# FRITO MISTO WITH
# CALABRIAN CHILE AIOLI

Serves 4 as an appetizer or light lunch

Vegetarian

Peanut, canola, or vegetable oil,
  for frying

1 cup rice flour

1 cup all-purpose flour

1 teaspoon baking powder

1/2 teaspoon kosher salt

2 cups chilled prosecco,
  Champagne, or club soda

1 pound nebrodini bianco
  mushrooms, halved and thinly
  sliced (6 to 8 cups)

1/2 fennel bulb, thinly sliced

1 small leek, white part only,
  trimmed, halved, and cleaned,
  slices separated

1 small zucchini, julienned

Flaky sea salt or coarse salt

1 fresh lemon, cut into wedges

Handful fresh herbs, such as
  basil or parsley

Calabrian Chile Aioli (opposite)
  or dipping sauce of choice,
  for serving

The perfect summer starter or light lunch—crispy, golden, frito misto! This popular Italian dish usually consists of meat or seafood and sliced vegetables dipped in a tempura-like batter and deep-fried. Nebrodini are the star in this one, and they fry up beautifully. I've added fennel, leeks, and zucchini. You could also use summer squash, sweet summer onion rings, broccoli, or green beans. Prosecco adds another layer of flavor to the batter. Substitute large oyster mushrooms if nebrodini aren't available.

Fill a medium heavy pot with about 4 inches of oil and set it over medium-high heat. Heat the oil to 350 degrees F.

In a large bowl, whisk together the rice flour, all-purpose flour, baking powder, and kosher salt. Pour in the prosecco and whisk lightly until just blended; do not overmix.

Place the sliced mushrooms, fennel, leek, and zucchini into a medium bowl. Working in batches, dip the mushrooms and vegetable slices, into the batter, shake off the excess, and fry in the oil for 1 to 3 minutes, or until golden and crisp. Using a spider spinner or a slotted spoon, transfer the mushrooms and vegetables to paper towels to drain, and lightly salt. Fry the herbs (see Note, page 103) and add them to the frito misto.

Serve with lemon wedges and aioli, or your favorite dipping sauce.

# CALABRIAN CHILE AIOLI

Makes about $^1/_2$ cup
Vegetarian

$^1/_2$ cup mayonnaise

1 tablespoon Calabrian chile paste

1 large garlic clove, grated

1 tablespoon fresh lemon juice

1 tablespoon white wine vinegar

$^1/_2$ teaspoon granulated sugar or honey

2 tablespoons olive oil

Kosher salt, to taste

This spicy, versatile aioli Is great on burgers or sandwiches too. Calabrian chiles have a heat level similar to cayenne pepper, slightly milder, but with a sweet, fruity flavor. If you can't find Calabrian chile paste, harissa or sriracha are both good substitutes.

In a small bowl, whisk together the mayonnaise, chile paste, garlic, lemon juice, vinegar, sugar, olive oil, and salt and chill until ready to use.

# OYSTER
## *Pleurotus ostreatus*

INTRODUCING a mushroom superhero! So many colors! Such a variety in one species! And a versatile and very edible mushroom that also contributes to a cleaner environment. What's not to like? It's at the top of my list of favorites and is beloved worldwide. From the large stemmed and glorious oyster royale to black pearls, blues, and grays, the bacon-flavored pinks, the delicate goldens, and the often seen—but never ordinary—pearl oyster. These popular mushrooms grow in clusters similar to oyster beds, which is how they earned their name.

They grow naturally on logs and dead or dying trees in shady spots, preferring hardwoods, especially aspen, beech, and oak, in subtropical and temperate forests worldwide.

Oyster mushrooms also have the ability to absorb and neutralize contaminated soil and are used industrially to soak toxic waste from damaged environments.

While extremely popular in Asian cuisines, oyster mushrooms are beloved worldwide for their sculptural beauty, delicate texture, and mild, savory flavor. The mushrooms typically have broad, thin, oyster- or fan-shaped caps and are white, gray, or tan, with gills lining the underside. The caps are sometimes frilly-edged and can be found in clusters of small mushrooms or individually as larger mushrooms.

## NUTRITIONAL VALUE

Of all mushrooms, oysters are the most protein-dense per weight. They contain immune-boosting beta-glucans and small but valuable amounts of lovastatin, an effective cholesterol-reducing compound.

They also have anti-inflammatory polysaccharides, folic acid, ample concentrations of B-complex vitamins, copper, iron, phosphorus, and vitamin D.

## SELECTION AND STORAGE

Look for mushrooms or clusters of mushrooms with a firm, slightly springy texture free of dark spots or damp, wilted edges.

Foraged oyster mushrooms usually don't need much cleaning. A quick wipe with a wet paper towel will usually do. Since purchased oyster mushrooms are usually cultivated, they can often be added straight into sauces without worry since they will likely be dirt-free.

The larger oyster mushrooms, black pearl, blue, gray, and ivory varieties store very well wrapped in paper towels, placed in paper bags and refrigerated.

Pink and yellow oysters have a short shelf life—two or three days at best. They need to retain moisture; refrigerate after wrapping them in paper towels and tucking them in open plastic freezer bags.

Oyster mushrooms will not freeze well raw. Cook them first before freezing, and they will store well for two to three months. Drying is a good option; they dry and rehydrate quickly due to their porous, spongy texture and add a soft, umami flavor to stocks and soups.

## COOKING METHODS

Braise, fry, grill, roast, sauté, stir-fry

## COOKING TIPS

Oyster mushrooms work well in a wide range of dishes. Black pearl oysters have a more intense flavor, while the flavor of other varieties such as pearl, blue, and gray is relatively subtle, less earthy than most other mushrooms, with a faint hint of anise. They soften beautifully in a slow braise or sauté and retain much of their texture when cooked on the grill or roasted.

The pink oyster cooks up with a bacon-like flavor and is delicious with egg dishes. The yellow oyster mushroom is uniquely delicate and a good stand-in for yellow foot chanterelles.

## FLAVOR PAIRINGS

- Beef
- Butter
- Cheese, Parmesan
- Chives
- Cream, cream sauces
- Eggs
- Fennel
- Garlic
- Onions
- Parsley
- Pasta
- Polenta
- Pork
- Rice
- Rosemary
- Sage
- Seafood
- Shallots
- Sherry
- Soy sauce
- Thyme
- Veal

# OYSTER MUSHROOM BOLOGNESE
# WITH PAPPARDELLE

1/4 cup dried porcini
    mushrooms

1 cup dry white wine

1 pound fresh oyster mush-
    rooms (6 to 8 cups) or 3 cups
    Duxelles (page 57)

2 tablespoons olive oil, plus
    more as needed

1 garlic clove, minced

1/2 small onion, finely chopped

1/3 fennel bulb, finely chopped
    (about 1/2 cup)

Pinch of kosher salt, plus
    2 teaspoons, divided, plus
    more as needed

Pinch of red pepper flakes

1/4 cup double-concentrated
    tomato paste

1 (16-ounce) can San Marzano
    tomatoes, puréed or passata

1/2 cup whole milk

2 tablespoons butter

1 (2-inch) piece Parmesan rind

Pinch of granulated sugar
    (optional)

12 ounces pappardelle, tagli-
    atelle, or bucatini

Freshly ground black pepper

1/2 cup grated Parmesan cheese,
    plus more for serving

This earthy, flavorful, and meatless bolognese sauce includes fresh oyster mushrooms and dried porcini. Substitute cremini, button, or any mild, fresh mushrooms. If you can't find dried porcini, dried shiitake are a good substitute. Adding a Parmesan cheese rind into the sauce is an insider Italian tip and a great addition to your repertoire. The cheese will add a creamy, nutty richness to most any sauce or soup.

Use good quality tomatoes, taste along the way, and adjust the seasoning. Butter (a tip from the Italian master, chef Marcella Hazan), adds a smooth decadence to the sauce.

---

In a small saucepan over medium heat, combine the dried porcini and wine and bring to a simmer, stirring occasionally, until the wine is reduced by half. Remove the pan from the heat and let the mushrooms steep while making the sauce.

Place the fresh oyster mushrooms in a food processor and pulse into 1/8- to 1/4-inch pieces or chop by hand.

Heat the oil in a large saucepan over medium-low heat. Add the garlic, onion, fennel, and pinch of salt and sauté for 5 to 7 minutes, or until softened. Raise the heat to medium, add the chopped oyster mushrooms, 1 teaspoon of salt, and cook, adding more oil if needed, for 7 to 8 minutes, until the mushrooms have released and reabsorbed their liquid. Add the pepper flakes and tomato paste and cook, stirring often, for an additional 4 to 5 minutes, or until the tomato paste has lost its bright color and the mushrooms are thoroughly coated.

Strain the porcini mushrooms from the wine and finely chop, reserving the liquid. Add the mushrooms, reserved soaking wine, puréed

tomatoes, and 1 teaspoon of salt to the saucepan. Stir in the milk, then the butter, and add the Parmesan rind. Turn the heat to medium-low and simmer, stirring often, for about 45 minutes. Taste the sauce while it cooks and add a pinch of sugar if the tomatoes are tart. The sauce should be thick and not runny, continue to cook if the sauce is too thin, add a little extra water (or mushroom stock if you have it on hand) if it's too thick.

While the sauce is simmering, bring a large pot of lightly salted water to a boil over medium-high heat. Add the pasta and cook according to the package instructions. (Drain, reserving 1 cup of the cooking water.) Toss the pasta with a little olive oil and set aside.

Taste the sauce, remove the Parmesan rind, adjust the seasoning with salt and pepper, and stir in the Parmesan cheese. To serve, divide the pasta among plates, spoon the sauce over the pasta, and top with additional cheese. (Alternatively, add the pasta to the skillet with the sauce and toss until the pasta is well coated, adding a little of the reserved pasta cooking water until it reaches your desired consistency. Serve with additional grated Parmesan cheese.)

# DUCK SAUSAGE AND OYSTER MUSHROOM POT PIE

2 tablespoons olive oil, plus more as needed

2 links (about 6 ounces) duck sausage

2 medium shallots, finely chopped

2 garlic cloves, minced

1 parsnip, diced

1 carrot, diced

1 celery stalk, diced

1$\frac{1}{2}$ teaspoons kosher salt, divided, plus more as needed

6 ounces oyster mushrooms, trimmed and cut into 2-inch pieces (about 3 cups)

2 tablespoons double-concentrated tomato paste

3 tablespoons rice flour, or all-purpose flour

2 tablespoons brandy

2 cups Roasted Mushroom Stock (page 232) or chicken stock, plus more as needed

2 or 3 thyme sprigs

Freshly ground black pepper

Cynthia's Pie Crust or 1 or 2 sheets all-butter pie dough, homemade or store-bought, prepared and chilled for at least 4 hours for a single-crust pie. For an optional double-crust pie, prebake the bottom crust.

1 large egg

1 tablespoon water

Rice flour gives the sauce a smooth texture for this hearty pot pie. Feel free to substitute your favorite mushroom for the oysters.

I recommend Cynthia's Pie Crust for this savory pie, but if you're short on time, use a store-bought pie dough. Make with either a single top layer or a double layer, with a bottom crust.

---

Heat the oil in a large saucepan over medium heat. Add the sausages and sauté for about 4 minutes, or until golden brown. Transfer to a cutting board, cut into $\frac{1}{2}$-inch slices, and transfer to a plate.

Add the shallots and garlic to the saucepan and sauté for 1 to 2 minutes. Add the parsnip, carrot, celery, and $\frac{1}{2}$ teaspoon of salt and cook, stirring often, for 5 to 6 minutes, or until just softened. Add the mushrooms and the remaining 1 teaspoon of salt, adding more oil if necessary, and cook, stirring occasionally, for 6 to 8 minutes, or until the mushrooms are golden.

Add the tomato paste and the cooked sausages and cook, stirring often, for 2 to 3 minutes, or until the tomato paste changes to a deeper color. Sprinkle the flour over the mixture and stir until coated. Add the brandy, wait a few seconds, and then stir in the stock. Add the thyme sprigs, partially cover, and cook at a low simmer, stirring often and adding more stock if needed, for 15 to 20 minutes, or until the vegetables are tender and the sauce has thickened.

Remove the pan from the heat. Taste, and adjust the seasoning with salt and pepper. Remove the thyme sprigs and let cool.

Preheat the oven to 425 degrees F and lightly grease a 9-inch pie pan for a single-crust pie (or have a prebaked pie crust ready for the optional double-crust pie). Mix the egg and water together.

Pour the mushroom mixture in the prepared pie pan and spread it out evenly. Place the rolled-out top crust over the mixture. Seal and crimp the edges and brush with the egg wash. Using a sharp knife, make at least 4 slits on the top to allow steam to escape. Bake for 30 to 40 minutes, or until the crust is golden and crispy.

# CYNTHIA'S PIE CRUST

Makes 2 pie crusts

Vegetarian

2 1/2 cups all-purpose flour, plus
more for rolling

1/2 teaspoon kosher salt

1 cup salted butter, diced into
1/2-inch cubes

8 to 10 tablespoons ice-cold
water

This is a fantastic, super-flaky pie dough recipe, generously shared by James Beard award–winning cookbook author Cynthia Graubart. It's perfect for this pot pie recipe and for the Chanterelle-Apricot Galette (page 79).

This makes enough for a double-crust 9-inch pie. Halve the recipe for a single-crust pie.

Place the flour and salt in the bowl of a food processor. Pulse 2 or 3 times to mix. Distribute the butter cubes evenly over the flour, and pulse 15 times. Add 4 tablespoons ice-cold water. Pulse 10 times. Add 4 more tablespoons ice-cold water and pulse 5 times. Using your fingers, squeeze a small amount of dough together. If it crumbles, add 1 to 2 more tablespoons of water to bring the dough together.

Turn the dough out onto a floured board and knead to form a cohesive dough. Divide the dough in half and form into 2 (5-inch) disks, wrap in plastic wrap, and refrigerate at least 1 hour.

Remove the disks from the refrigerator and let rest for 10 minutes before using.

Preheat the oven to 425 degrees F.

Flour a work surface and rolling pin. Rolling from the center out to the edge, continue rolling the disk, turning the dough a quarter turn after each roll, until the dough is roughly 1 inch larger than the pie pan. Repeat and make the top crust with the remaining dough.

Line a pie pan with 1 of the rolled-out pieces of pie dough. Place a sheet of parchment paper on the bottom crust and fill with pie weights or dried beans. Place on a baking sheet and bake for 10 to 15 minutes. Take out of the oven, remove the parchment and pie weights, and bake for an additional 15 minutes, or until cooked through. Cool before using.

# BAKED OYSTER MUSHROOMS À LA SAVOYARDE

1 tablespoon grapeseed or another neutral oil

3 tablespoons butter, divided

3 shallots, peeled and thinly sliced crosswise

8 ounces chopped oyster mushrooms (about 4 cups)

1 teaspoon kosher salt

2 tablespoons brandy or Kirsch

1 1/2 tablespoons all-purpose flour

1/2 cup half-and-half

1/8 cup crème fraîche

2/3 cup grated cheese, such as Gruyère, raclette, or Jarlsberg, divided

1 tablespoon minced fresh parsley

Mushrooms Savoyarde, a classic French mushroom preparation, is a creamy spread of chopped, sautéed mushrooms, cream, and cheese. It is usually served with bread or crackers. Baking the mushrooms with a layer of cheese on top transforms it into a bubbly hot, memorable appetizer for dipping toasted bread or as a topping for cooked potatoes or vegetables.

Substitute your favorite mushroom or a variety of mushrooms for the oyster mushrooms.

Heat the oil and 1 tablespoon of the butter in a large skillet or saucepan over medium heat. Add the shallots and cook for 3 to 4 minutes, or until softened. Increase the heat to medium-high, add 1 tablespoon of butter, and sauté the mushrooms, adding the salt as the mushrooms begin to color. When the mushrooms are golden brown, add the brandy, then stir in the flour and the remaining 1 tablespoon of butter. Stir until the mixture is well coated. Add the half-and-half and crème fraîche and stir until smooth. Bring to a simmer and then remove from the heat and stir in 1/3 cup of the cheese. The mixture will be thick and gooey.

Preheat the oven to broil.

Transfer the mixture to a small baking dish and sprinkle with the remaining 1/3 cup of cheese. Broil for 3 to 5 minutes, or until the top is golden brown.

Sprinkle with parsley and serve.

# DUCK FAT-ROASTED OYSTER MUSHROOMS WITH FRESH HERBS AND SMOKED SALT

Serves 2 to 3

2 tablespoons duck fat, plus
more as needed

8 ounces thick-sliced oyster
mushrooms (about 4 cups)

Coarse smoked sea salt

Fresh lemon juice, for seasoning

Chopped fresh parsley, for
garnish

1 cup microgreens, for serving
(optional)

Duck fat and mushrooms are a flavorful pairing for roasting, and a sprinkle of smoked salt is the perfect finish. Almost any hearty mushroom will work well in this side dish recipe.

Preheat the oven to 425 degrees F.

Heat the duck fat in a large, oven-safe skillet over medium-high heat. Add the mushrooms and sauté, thoroughly coating with the duck fat, for 3 to 4 minutes to lightly sear.

Transfer the skillet to the oven and roast for 8 to 10 minutes, stirring halfway through the cooking time, until the mushrooms turn a deep caramel brown. Remove from the oven and sprinkle with the smoked sea salt, a spritz of fresh lemon juice, and chopped fresh parsley. Serve by themselves or over a bed of microgreens tossed with a squeeze of fresh lemon.

# BLACK PEARL OYSTER MUSHROOM STROGANOFF

Serves 4

1/2 medium onion, thinly sliced

2 tablespoons olive oil, divided

1/2 teaspoon kosher salt, plus
    more as needed

2 small black garlic cloves

2 cups Roasted Mushroom
    Stock (page 232), chicken
    stock, or vegetable stock,
    divided

Freshly ground black pepper

8 to 10 ounces boneless ribeye,
    cut into 2 × 1/2-inch slices

2 tablespoons butter

12 ounces black pearl oyster
    mushrooms, trimmed and
    sliced (5 to 6 cups)

2 tablespoons double-
    concentrated tomato paste

1/2 cup white wine

2 thyme sprigs

12 ounces wide egg noodles or
    pappardelle

1 teaspoon Dijon mustard

1/3 cup crème fraîche

1/3 cup sour cream

2 tablespoons chopped fresh
    parsley

Black pearl oysters are a cross between the king oyster and blue oyster mushrooms, with the deep umami flavor from trumpet mushrooms, and a meaty but tender oyster texture from cap to stem. In this recipe, these hearty mushrooms pair with a rich, creamy, black garlic–sour cream sauce, and roasted sweet Vidalia onions. Serve over wide egg noodles, pappardelle, fettuccine, rice, or mashed potatoes. This would also be terrific over grits. Try making it with other earthy mushroom varieties too, including portobellos, cremini, or shiitake.

---

Preheat the oven to 425 degrees F.

On a baking sheet, toss together the onion slices, 1 tablespoon of olive oil, and salt. Roast for 12 to 15 minutes, or until the onion is softened and the edges are beginning to char; set aside.

In a blender or food processor, purée the black garlic and 1/2 cup of the mushroom stock until smooth; set aside.

Lightly season the ribeye with salt and pepper. Heat the remaining 1 tablespoon of olive oil in a large skillet over high heat, place the beef in the skillet, quickly sear, and then transfer to a plate.

Lower the heat to medium-high and add the butter. When the butter foams, add the mushrooms to the skillet and sauté (in batches if necessary) for 8 to 10 minutes, or until nicely caramelized. Stir in the onion, the beef, and tomato paste and cook for 1 to 2 minutes, or until the tomato paste has darkened. Add the wine and continue to cook for 1 to 2 minutes until the liquid is reduced by half.

Stir in the remaining 1 1/2 cups of stock, the black garlic–stock mixture, and the thyme sprigs. Turn the heat to medium-low and simmer, stirring often, for 15 to 20 minutes, or until the beef is tender and the sauce is

reduced and has thickened slightly. Taste, and adjust the seasoning with salt and pepper.

While the beef is simmering, bring a large pot of lightly salted water to a boil over medium-high heat. Add the egg noodles and cook for 8 to 10 minutes, or until al dente. Drain and set aside.

Stir the mustard, crème fraîche, and sour cream into the beef mixture and simmer (do not boil) for an additional 3 to 4 minutes, or until the sauce is smooth and thickened. Stir in the pasta and toss until well coated. Taste, adjust the seasoning, if needed, with salt and pepper, sprinkle with parsley, and serve.

# PINK OYSTER CARBONARA

2 tablespoons butter

8 ounces pink oyster mushrooms, trimmed and thinly sliced (about 4 cups)

1/2 teaspoon kosher salt, plus more as needed

1/4 teaspoon dried crushed rosemary

1/8 teaspoon dried rubbed sage

1/2 garlic clove, grated

12 ounces dried spaghetti

2 whole eggs plus 2 egg yolks, at room temperature

1/3 cup grated aged Parmesan, plus more for serving

1/3 cup grated Pecorino Romano, plus more for serving

Freshly ground black pepper

Pink oyster mushrooms have a delicate bacon-like flavor, and with an added touch of herbs and garlic, make a pretty good, mushroom-guanciale substitute in this creamy carbonara. Use good quality dried pasta and aged cheese for the best results.

Melt the butter in a large saucepan over medium-high heat. Add the mushrooms and sauté for 3 to 4 minutes. Add the salt, rosemary, sage, and garlic, stir thoroughly, then leave alone to cook, stirring occasionally, for another 2 to 3 minutes, or until lightly browned and crispy. Remove from the heat.

Bring a large pot of lightly salted water to a boil over medium-high heat. Add the spaghetti and cook for 8 to 10 minutes, or until al dente. Drain, reserving 1 cup of the cooking water.

In a medium bowl, whisk together the eggs, egg yolks, and cheeses. Add 1/3 cup of the reserved pasta water and whisk until smooth.

Return the saucepan to the stove over low heat. Add the hot pasta and the egg mixture to the mushrooms and vigorously toss everything together, adding more pasta water if needed to create a creamy sauce. Taste, and adjust the seasoning with salt and lots of pepper. Shower with a good handful of additional grated cheese before serving.

# PIOPPINO

*Agrocybe aegerita*

# OH, THE PIOPPINO!

A mushroom worth knowing. Also referred to as the velvet pioppino, these amazing mushrooms have been growing since ancient times. Native to Asia, pioppino mushrooms are widely cultivated and found in local markets and specialty grocers nearly worldwide. Cultivating kits are also available online. Pioppini are easy and fun to grow and usually produce multiple fruitings.

You will find pioppino mushrooms in the wild in southern Europe, Asia, Australia, Mexico, and in the southeastern United States, summer through fall, on the logs and stumps of deciduous trees. Hard to miss, they form large clusters near poplar, willow, box elder, maple, and elm trees. The mushrooms are small to medium in size, with round caps that flatten as they grow, perched on top of thin, elegant, cream-colored stems.

## NUTRITIONAL VALUE

In China, pioppini are known and used for their anti-inflammatory and antifungal properties. Pioppino mushrooms are rich in copper, fiber, and vitamin B5 and contain potassium, biotin, folate, iron, selenium, and vitamins B2 and B3. Like other mushrooms, the pioppino is low in cholesterol and fat, high in fiber, and a good protein source, containing all the essential amino acids.

## SELECTION AND STORAGE

Pioppino mushrooms are tender and at their very best when young. Choose mushrooms with still-rounded caps if available. Avoid any that have begun to wilt or have spots or mushy areas on the caps or stems. The stems become tough as they age, the caps will still be delicious—just give a quick trim to the stems and save for stocks.

Pioppino mushrooms store well. Placed in the refrigerator with a good wrap in paper towels and placed in an open plastic storage bag, these mushrooms should keep fresh for days.

## COOKING METHODS

Braise, pickle, roast, sauté, stir-fry, and add to soups

## COOKING TIPS

Pioppini are prolific growers and are strikingly beautiful. They have a sweet, almost floral aroma, and their flavor is a bit peppery and earthy, but not too much so. They are the close in flavor to the porcini.

Their texture remains slightly firm after cooking, making a nice textural contrast in soups and stews, and they work nicely in pasta and rice dishes. An excellent stand-in for meat in vegan or vegetable stir-fries, they are the perfect choice for pickling or for sautéing in olive oil or butter.

## FLAVOR PAIRINGS

- Arugula
- Barley
- Beef
- Butter
- Cheese: goat, Parmesan
- Chives
- Eggs
- Game
- Garlic
- Hazelnuts
- Lettuce, radicchio
- Marjoram
- Onions
- Parsley
- Pasta
- Polenta
- Potatoes
- Quinoa
- Spinach
- Tarragon
- Tomato
- Vinegar, pickling
- Walnuts

# PIOPPINO POUTINE

## PIOPPINO SAUCE

3 tablespoons butter, divided

1 large shallot, thinly sliced crosswise

1 large garlic clove, minced

8 ounces pioppino mushrooms, trimmed, large mushrooms halved lengthwise (about 4 cups)

Pinch of kosher salt, plus more as needed

1 tablespoon double-concentrated tomato paste

2 tablespoons Marsala wine

3 1/2 cups Roasted Mushroom Stock (page 232) or a combination of low-sodium chicken stock and beef stock, divided

2 tablespoons cornstarch

Freshly ground black pepper

Pioppino mushrooms in a rich brown gravy ladled over crispy french fries and topped with melty cheddar cheese curds, what's not to like? Cheese curds are worth the extra effort to find for this mushroom variation of the popular Canadian dish (although you may just find them at your local grocery). In a pinch, use whole-milk mozzarella torn into bite-size chunks. Substitute any mushroom of choice. Find some good frozen fries if you don't have time to make them from scratch.

---

**TO MAKE THE SAUCE,** heat 1 tablespoon of butter in a medium saucepan over medium heat. Add the shallot and sauté for 2 to 3 minutes, or until softened. Add the garlic and cook, stirring, for 1 minute.

Add the remaining 2 tablespoons of butter to the pan, stir in the mushrooms, and sauté for 4 to 5 minutes, or until golden, adding a pinch of salt halfway through the cooking time. Add the tomato paste,

## FRENCH FRIES

2 pounds russet or Yukon gold
potatoes, peeled and cut
lengthwise into ½-inch-wide
fries, soaked in ice water
for at least 1 hour, and up to
24 hours, prior to frying

Peanut or vegetable oil, for
frying

Kosher salt

## TO SERVE

2 cups cheddar cheese curds

2 tablespoons chopped fresh
parsley

stir, and cook for 1 to 2 minutes. Whisk in the Marsala and 3 cups of the stock, and simmer for 15 minutes. The sauce should be reduced and the mushrooms tender.

In a small bowl, whisk together the cornstarch and remaining ½ cup of stock until smooth to make a slurry. Stir the slurry into the mushroom mixture and continue to simmer for 2 to 3 minutes, or until the sauce has thickened. (Add water if the sauce becomes too thick.) Taste and adjust the seasoning with salt and pepper. Remove from the heat, cover, and keep warm while making the fries.

**TO MAKE THE FRIES,** drain the potatoes well and pat dry. Line a baking sheet with paper towels.

Heat 3 inches of oil in a heavy pot over medium-high heat to 350 degrees F. Add the potatoes to the oil and fry for 6 to 8 minutes, or until they begin to turn a very light golden color. Using a slotted strainer, transfer the potatoes to the baking sheet to drain.

Raise the oil temperature to 375 degrees F. Add the fried potatoes to the pot again and fry for 6 to 8 minutes, or until golden brown. Transfer the fries to the baking sheet to drain, and season immediately with salt. Keep them warm in a low oven.

**TO SERVE,** arrange the fries on a serving platter or plates.

Return the saucepan with the sauce to the stove over medium heat. Add the cheese curds and cover the pan with a lid for 3 to 4 minutes, or just until the curds begin to melt. Remove the pan from the heat and spoon the sauce over the hot fries. Toss with the gravy to coat.

(Alternatively, spoon the gravy over the fries, top with the cheese curds and bake in a preheated 300-degree F oven for 3 to 5 minutes, or until the curds begin to melt.)

Garnish with chopped parsley and serve.

# PAN-ROASTED PHEASANT AND PIOPPINO RAGU

**BRINE**

6 cups water

$\frac{1}{3}$ cup salt

2 tablespoons granulated sugar

2 bay leaves

$\frac{1}{2}$ onion, sliced

2 garlic cloves, crushed

1 (2-pound) pheasant, farm
raised or wild

Golden pan-roasted pheasant pairs with sweet pearl onions and earthy pioppini in a rich Madeira-laced ragu. A quick brine will ensure a moist and tasty bird—nothing fancy, just a saltwater bath with a touch of sugar and a bay leaf or two.

Pioppino mushroom stems tend to toughen as they mature, harvest your pioppini early while the caps are still rounded and the stems tender. You can substitute any favorite mushroom in this recipe.

**TO MAKE THE BRINE,** in a large stockpot over medium-high heat, bring the water to a boil, add the salt, sugar, and bay leaves. Stir until the sugar and salt have dissolved. Add the onion and garlic. Remove from the heat. When the brine is cool, add the pheasant and refrigerate overnight. When you're ready to cook, remove the pheasant from the brine, pat dry, and cut into quarters.

**MUSHROOM STOCK**

2 cups water

1/4 ounce dried porcini
    mushrooms

**RAGU**

2 tablespoons butter or ghee

2 tablespoons grapeseed oil or
    olive oil

Coarse salt

1 cup frozen pearl onions,
    thawed

2 garlic cloves, minced

6 ounces pioppino mushrooms,
    tough stem ends trimmed
    and larger mushrooms halved
    (about 5 cups)

1 teaspoon kosher salt, plus
    more as needed

2 tablespoons double-
    concentrated tomato paste

1/2 cup dry white wine

1 1/2 cups Mushroom Stock

Freshly ground black pepper

2 or 3 thyme sprigs

1/4 cup Madeira wine

1 tablespoon cornstarch

2 tablespoons water

Chopped fresh parsley, for
    garnish (optional)

Prepared mashed potatoes or
    egg noodles, for serving

**TO MAKE THE MUSHROOM STOCK,** in a small saucepan over medium-high heat, bring the water to a simmer. Add the mushrooms and simmer for 5 to 6 minutes; cover and steep for 20 minutes. Strain the stock and chop and reserve the mushrooms.

Preheat the oven to 325 degrees F.

**TO MAKE THE RAGU,** heat the butter and oil in an extra-large, covered saucepan over medium-high heat until foaming. Sprinkle the pheasant quarters generously with coarse salt, add to the pan, and sauté, turning occasionally, until lightly browned on all sides. Transfer to a plate and set aside.

Add the onions to the pan, quickly sear for 2 to 3 minutes, then add the garlic and stir and cook for an additional minute until softened (do not brown). Add the mushrooms, sprinkle with the kosher salt, toss in the pan, and cook briefly to sear, about 2 minutes. Add the tomato paste, stirring to coat the mushrooms and onions. Cook for 2 to 3 minutes until the paste has deepened in color. Pour in the white wine and reduce by half. Stir in the stock and reserved mushrooms, then taste and season with salt and pepper. Add the pheasant quarters, skin side up, and the thyme sprigs and cover the pan. Place in the oven and roast for 20 to 25 minutes, or until cooked through and tender.

Remove the pan from the oven, transfer the pheasant to a platter or serving dish, cover, and keep warm.

Place the pan over medium heat, stir in the Madeira, and bring to a simmer. Whisk together the cornstarch and water, add to the pan, whisk, then stir until the sauce has thickened, 3 to 4 minutes. Remove the thyme sprigs, taste, and season with salt and pepper.

**TO SERVE,** spoon the ragu over the pheasant quarters, top with a sprinkle of fresh parsley (if using), and serve with mashed potatoes or egg noodles.

# PIOPPINO AND BARLEY STEW

2 tablespoons olive oil

1 medium leek, ends trimmed, white and pale green parts only, halved lengthwise, cleaned, and then cut into ¼-inch half-rounds (about 1 cup)

4 ounces pioppino mushrooms, stems trimmed and halved (about 2 cups)

½ teaspoon kosher salt, plus more as needed

1 garlic clove, minced

1 cup tomato juice

4 cups Mushroom Stock (page 191), chicken stock, or vegetable broth

1 cup pearl barley

1 teaspoon dried oregano

1 bay leaf

1 (2-inch) Parmesan rind plus grated Parmesan cheese for finishing (optional)

3 cups fresh spinach, torn into bite-size pieces

Freshly ground black pepper

This chilly night favorite is rich with healthy, nutty barley, pioppino mushrooms, and fresh spinach. Bring out the crusty garlic bread and pour a nice glass of red wine.

Heat the oil in a large pot or Dutch oven over medium heat. Add the leek and sauté for about 3 minutes, or until softened. Add the mushrooms and the salt, and sauté for 4 to 5 minutes, or until the mushrooms begin to caramelize. Add the garlic and stir briefly. Add the tomato juice, mushroom stock, barley, oregano, and bay leaf and bring to a boil. Turn the heat to low, add the Parmesan rind, cover, and simmer, stirring occasionally, for 15 to 20 minutes, or until the barley is almost tender.

Remove the lid and continue to cook for an additional 10 to 15 minutes, or until the barley is completely tender. Stir in the spinach and cook for 3 to 4 minutes, or until wilted. Remove the bay leaf and Parmesan rind, and adjust the seasoning with salt and pepper.

Serve with grated Parmesan cheese.

# PICKLED PIOPPINI

Makes about 4 cups

Vegan

²/₃ cups granulated sugar

1 cup tamari or low-sodium soy
    sauce

1 ¹/₈ cups rice wine vinegar

6 or 7 crushed Szechuan
    peppercorns

6 fresh thin peeled ginger slices

2 cups water

12 ounces whole pioppino
    mushrooms, tough ends
    trimmed (about 4 cups)

1 tablespoon toasted sesame
    seeds

This is a fantastic pickling recipe adapted from one by Iron Chef contestant Chef Duskie Estes. If you don't have pioppini, try beech, button, cremini, or hedgehog mushrooms, all of which would be good stand-ins. Cut larger mushrooms in half.

In a nonreactive saucepan over medium-high heat, bring the sugar, tamari, vinegar, peppercorns, ginger, and water to a boil. Place the mushrooms in a quart-size jar with a lid, pour the pickling liquid over the mushrooms, and stir in the sesame seeds. The mushrooms should be covered in the liquid, if not add a little extra water. They're ready to eat once cooled. Store in an airtight container in the refrigerator for up to 1 month.

# PORCINI
## *Boletus edulis*

**THE INFAMOUS** and often elusive porcini, or "piglets" as they are often fondly referred to by Italians, have long been cherished among chefs and mushroom connoisseurs worldwide for their intense, nutty flavor and attractive, stately appearance.

Porcini are mycorrhizal mushrooms found in the late summer and fall near the roots of oak trees or next to conifers like spruce, pine, firs, and even hemlocks. Easily identifiable with brown, slightly sticky caps and spongy undersides, set atop thick, sturdy white stems, they tend to grow in groups and prefer sunny locations. Look for them in the open areas of the woods.

## NUTRITIONAL VALUE
Porcini mushrooms are another mushroom containing significant amounts of protein. They are also a good source of A, C, and B vitamins, copper, potassium, zinc, and selenium.

## SELECTION AND STORAGE
Porcini are unable to be cultivated, so unless you find them through foraging locally, be prepared to pay a high price for purchasing them fresh through specialty retailers. Fresh, frozen, and dried porcini are usually available online.

If you are a lucky hunter and find porcini, use them within a couple of days, as they do not store well. Wrapping them in paper towels in an open plastic bag in the refrigerator should keep them reasonably fresh for two to three days. A better option is to freeze them. Cut them into pieces or slices and freeze them directly on a sheet pan before sealing them in freezer containers or bags and storing. They should last for up to four months. Blanching them before storing in the freezer will extend their quality for up to one year.

Drying is likely your best option; dried porcini pack a lot of flavor and are invaluable in your pantry. Rehydrate them in warm stock, water, or wine until softened, then strain and keep the soaking water to add to broths or sauces. The rehydrated mushrooms can then be chopped and sautéed and added to your dish.

## COOKING METHODS
Fry, grill, roast, sauté, and add to risottos, soups, and stews

## COOKING TIPS
One of the ultimate mushrooms to cook with, count on porcini to elevate any dish you use them in! Porcini mushrooms are earthy with a strong nutty, slightly peppery flavor and have a tender but still meaty texture when cooked. They are a delicious addition to risotto and pasta dishes, pair well with steaks and roasted chicken, and are sublime simply sautéed in butter.

Clean your porcini mushrooms with a brush or damp paper towel before use. Avoid using too much water.

## FLAVOR PAIRINGS

- Almonds
- Bacon
- Beef
- Brandy
- Butter
- Carrots
- Cheese: fontina, Parmesan
- Chicken
- Cream
- Eggs
- Fennel
- Fish, white
- French cuisine
- Garlic
- Hazelnuts
- Italian cuisine
- Lemon
- Madeira
- Olive oil
- Onions
- Parsley
- Pasta
- Pepper, black
- Polenta
- Pork
- Potatoes
- Shallots
- Sherry
- Spinach
- Steak
- Thyme
- Tomatoes: fresh, sun-dried
- Wine, dry white

# PORK AND PORCINI RAGU
# WITH PACCHERI

Serves 3 to 4

⅓ to ½ ounce dried porcini mushrooms (about ⅓ cup)

1½ cups Roasted Mushroom Stock (page 232) or chicken stock

3 tablespoons olive oil, divided

8 ounces cooked roasted pork shoulder or country ribs, cut into ½ × ¾-inch pieces

Kosher salt as needed, plus 1 teaspoon

Freshly ground black pepper

¼ medium onion, finely chopped

2 garlic cloves, minced

4 ounces finely chopped fresh porcini mushrooms, or cremini or shiitake mushrooms (about 2 cups)

2 tablespoons double-concentrated tomato paste

⅓ cup red wine

1 (14-ounce) can plum tomatoes, with juice

1 teaspoon dried oregano

Pinch of red pepper flakes

12 ounces dried paccheri, rigatoni, or penne pasta

½ cup grated Grana Padano or Parmesan cheese, plus more for serving

2 tablespoons chopped fresh herbs, such as basil and/or flat-leaf parsley

Extra-virgin olive oil or butter, for finishing

This is a delicious and simple ragu using flavorful roasted pork and dry red wine. Earthy porcini stock gives the sauce depth of flavor. The combination of rich pork and sour-sweet San Marzano tomatoes create a beautiful sauce over big tubes of paccheri pasta. Substitute cremini or even shiitake for fresh porcini, and any hearty tube pasta will work. Use freshly grated cheese and a good olive oil. Quality ingredients are key.

In a medium, heavy saucepan or Dutch oven over medium heat, combine the dried porcini and stock and gently simmer for 20 minutes. Remove and strain the mushrooms, reserving the cooking liquid. Chop the mushrooms and set aside.

Add 2 tablespoons of olive oil to the saucepan and raise the heat to medium-high. Season the pork lightly with salt and pepper, place in the pan, and sauté for 5 to 6 minutes, stirring occasionally, or until lightly browned. Stir in the onion and garlic, and sauté for 2 to 3 minutes, or until softened. Add the fresh and the reserved rehydrated porcini with a good pinch of salt and the remaining 1 tablespoon of oil. Sauté for 5 to 6 minutes, or until golden brown. Stir in the tomato paste, coating the pork and vegetables, and cook for 2 to 3 minutes, or until the paste has darkened. Add the wine and cook for 1 to 2 minutes until reduced by half.

Turn the heat to medium-low, add the reserved mushroom liquid, tomatoes, oregano, 1 teaspoon of salt, and the pepper flakes. Simmer, breaking up the tomatoes with a wooden spoon, for 15 to 20 minutes, stirring occasionally and adding water as necessary. Taste the sauce and adjust the seasoning if needed with additional salt and pepper. Cover and remove from the heat.

Bring a large pot of lightly salted water to a boil over medium-high heat. Add the pasta and cook for 7 to 10 minutes, or until al dente. Drain, reserving 1 cup of the cooking water.

Place the pan over medium heat, toss the pasta with the sauce, adding the reserved water, a little at a time, until the sauce is beautifully blended with the pasta. Stir in the cheese and herbs. Finish with additional cheese and a drizzle of extra-virgin olive oil.

# PORCINI AND CHESTNUT PÂTÉ

2 tablespoons butter or
  neutral oil

1 large shallot, minced

1 large garlic clove, minced

4 ounces finely chopped fresh
  porcini mushrooms (about 2
  cups)

$^1/_2$ teaspoon kosher salt, plus
  more as needed

$^1/_3$ cup roasted skinless
  chestnuts

2 tablespoons brandy

3 tablespoons crème fraîche

2 teaspoons chopped fresh
  tarragon leaves

Freshly ground black pepper

Crackers or toasted bread
  slices, for serving

Chestnuts add a depth of sweetness and pair beautifully with the porcini in this decadent pâté. Try adding it to a charcuterie board with bread or crackers or tuck a small amount under the skin of chicken breasts or thighs before roasting. Frozen porcini are a good stand-in for fresh.

Heat the butter in a medium saucepan over medium heat. Add the shallot and garlic and sauté for 4 to 5 minutes, or until softened. Add the mushrooms and sauté, adding the salt halfway through, for 5 to 6 minutes, or until fully cooked and any liquid released is reabsorbed. Stir in the chestnuts, add the brandy, and cook for 1 to 2 minutes, until the liquid is absorbed. Remove the pan from the heat and stir in the crème fraîche and tarragon. Taste and adjust the seasoning with salt and pepper. Transfer the mixture to a food processor and blend until smooth. Serve with crackers or toasted bread.

# PORCINI AND
# POTATO CHOWDER

Serves 4

Vegetarian

3 1/2 cups vegetable stock or
    chicken stock, plus more
    as needed

1/2 ounce dried porcini mush-
    rooms (about 1/3 cup)

2 tablespoons butter

1 tablespoon olive oil

2 garlic cloves, minced

1/2 onion, diced

1 celery stalk, diced

1/4 cup diced fennel

1 teaspoon kosher salt, plus
    more as needed

1/4 teaspoon freshly ground
    black pepper, plus more as
    needed

1 ounce sliced fresh porcini,
    cremini, or shiitake mush-
    rooms (about 1 cup)

1 tablespoon medium or dry
    sherry, such as Amontillado

2 tablespoons rice flour

1 large russet potato, peeled
    and diced (about 1 1/2 cups)

2 thyme sprigs

1/2 cup heavy cream

Chopped fresh herbs, such as
    parsley, tarragon, or chives

This is a rich, creamy, and comforting chowder full of porcini-style umami flavor, and perfect for chilly weather. Substitute other mushrooms if porcini are unavailable. Rice flour adds a special smoothness to the sauce, but use all-purpose flour if you don't have it on hand. Don't skimp on the sherry—use a good quality drinking sherry or skip this step.

In a medium saucepan over medium heat, bring the stock to a simmer. Add the dried porcini and simmer gently for about 20 minutes, until the mushrooms are softened. Strain, reserve the liquid, and chop the mushrooms, then set aside.

Heat the butter and olive oil in a medium pot or Dutch oven over medium-low heat. Add the garlic, onion, celery, fennel, salt, and pepper and sauté for 3 to 4 minutes, or until just softened. Stir in the fresh mushrooms and cook until golden and tender. (Remove a few slices for garnish if you like, set aside, and keep warm.) Stir in the sherry and sprinkle the rice flour over the vegetables. Add the reserved stock and bring to a boil, stirring constantly. Stir in the potato, the reserved rehydrated porcini, and the thyme sprigs. Cover and simmer, stirring occasionally, for about 25 minutes, or until the vegetables are tender. Add additional stock or water if needed.

Remove the lid, stir in the cream, and cook for 5 to 6 more minutes, or until the chowder has a creamy, thick consistency. Taste, and adjust the seasoning with additional salt and pepper. To serve, spoon into bowls and top with chopped fresh herbs and/or the reserved mushroom slices.

REISHI

*Ganoderma lucidum*

REISHI, also known as lingzhi, are fascinating and hard to miss. Kidney-shaped fungi with colored bands on long stems, growing at the base of aged maple trees, is a rare and fascinating sight. Only about three out of ten thousand trees will have lingzhi arising from natural wild growth. Despite its relative rarity in the wild, reishi is easily cultivated on hardwood logs, sawdust, or wood chips.

## NUTRITIONAL VALUE

The reishi mushroom is among several medicinal mushrooms that have been popular in Asia for centuries. Historically used for infections, they are believed to relieve fatigue and lower blood sugar and blood pressure. Reishi mushrooms are adaptogens—plants that help combat stress. These mushrooms also have anticancer and anti-inflammatory properties and enhance immune function. Further research is needed to determine the safety and effectiveness of reishi as an adjunctive cancer treatment.

Please consult your doctor before consuming any mushroom for medicinal purposes, especially if you already take medications.

## COOKING METHODS

Powders, teas, and tinctures

## COOKING TIPS

This mushroom is almost inedible, but is valuable for its health benefits in teas, tinctures, and powders. If using in teas, be creative and add fruit or herb tea leaves for a more flavorful tea.

# REISHI AND HONEY TEA

4 cups water

5 to 6 grams (about 3 [2-inch] pieces) dried reishi or 25 grams fresh

Grated zest of $\frac{1}{2}$ lemon

2 tablespoons honey or agave syrup, plus more as needed

$\frac{1}{2}$ lemon, cut into wedges

This makes a mild, lemony tea.

In a medium saucepan with a lid over medium-high heat, bring the water to a boil. Add the reishi, lemon zest, and honey and stir to combine. Turn the heat to medium-low, cover, and simmer for 2 to 3 hours, or until the flavor has developed to your taste. Strain the tea before drinking. Add more honey and a squeeze of lemon juice to finish.

# REISHI-RASPBERRY ICED TEA

9 cups water, divided

5 to 6 grams dried reishi (about 2 tablespoons), crushed

2 tablespoons loose dried raspberry leaves

2 tablespoons honey or agave syrup

3 tablespoons granulated sugar, divided

$2\frac{1}{2}$ cups fresh raspberries, divided

1 lemon, cut into slices

Fresh mint leaves, for garnish (optional)

A bright, colorful, and refreshing tea, this has the health benefits of both reishi mushrooms and raspberries. You will need a tea-ball infuser and a fine-mesh strainer for the finished tea.

In a medium saucepan with a lid over medium-high heat, bring 5 cups of the water to a boil. Add the reishi pieces. Place the raspberry leaves in a tea-ball infuser and add it to the saucepan.

Turn the heat to medium-low, cover, and simmer for 30 minutes. Remove the tea ball. Add the honey and 2 tablespoons of the sugar, and continue to simmer, uncovered, for an additional $1\frac{1}{2}$ hours, until reduced to about 2 cups. Strain through a fine-mesh strainer and let cool.

In a medium saucepan over medium heat, combine 2 cups of the raspberries, the remaining 4 cups of water, and the remaining 1 tablespoon of sugar and mix well. Simmer, mashing occasionally with a fork or spoon, for 15 to 20 minutes. Strain through a fine-mesh strainer and cool.

Pour the raspberry juice and reishi tea into a pitcher. Add a few lemon slices and most of the remaining $1/2$ cup of fresh raspberries. Serve in tall glasses over ice and garnish with lemon slices, raspberries, and mint leaves (if using).

# SHIITAKE
## *Lentinula edodes*

**SHIITAKE MUSHROOMS** are one of the most versatile and popular mushrooms in the world. Native to East Asia, they are also the world's oldest cultivated mushroom. A staple in Asian cuisine, they are consumed both fresh and dried. These delicious mushrooms integrate well into most dishes, and their earthy essence is invaluable for adding extra umami flavor. You will likely find shiitake in your local supermarket or in Asian markets.

Chabana donko or donko shiitake, also known as flower mushrooms, are the most sought-after premium shiitake and are slightly larger and even more intense in flavor. Considered winter mushrooms, their slower growth, paired with moisture and temperature changes, create distinctive crackled tops during cultivation. The cracks add a unique beauty to the mushrooms. Although fresh donko are harder to come by, (you may find them online) dried donko mushrooms can usually be found in Asian markets. When reconstituted, they produce a rich, intensely flavored umami broth.

## NUTRITIONAL VALUE

Shiitake mushrooms are high in potassium, B vitamins, iron, magnesium, copper, selenium, and zinc. The protein found in shiitake mushrooms contains all nine essential amino acids and is considered a complete protein, with high amounts of leucine and lysine and ergothioneine, also known as a longevity vitamin.

They also have a deep umami-rich flavor and a meaty texture, another reason vegetarians and vegans are drawn to shiitake as a meat substitute.

## SELECTION AND STORAGE

Look for shiitakes with firm, rounded caps with the edges rolled downward toward tight gills. The stems should be white and firm, with caps free of blemishes.

For short-term storage, wrap the mushrooms in paper towels and then place them inside an open plastic storage bag. To freeze, cook the mushrooms in a sauce first, store them in an airtight container, and freeze for up to six months. For ideal long-term storage, these mushrooms dry very well, which has the added benefit of concentrating their already deep umami flavor even more—you'll enjoy having them in your pantry!

## COOKING METHODS

Braise, grill, roast, sauté, stew, stir-fry, add to soups

## COOKING TIPS

Remove the stems before cooking, save and freeze them for use in stocks. Shiitake are at home in Asian broths and soups, and when sautéed make a terrific accompaniment for burgers and steak, and are luxuriously good served over pasta with a bit of added cream.

You can't ask for a better-tasting mushroom, even if simply sautéed in butter with a splash of wine and a sprinkling of fresh herbs. Try roasting them in olive oil and fresh garlic to top a slice or two of toasted, crusty bread.

## FLAVOR PAIRINGS

- Asparagus
- Bacon
- Basil
- Beef
- Bell peppers
- Broccoli
- Cheese, Parmesan
- Cream
- Eggplant
- Garlic
- Leek
- Parsley
- Polenta
- Rice
- Rosemary
- Scallions
- Sesame
- Soba
- South Asian cuisine
- Soy
- Vinegar: balsamic, sherry
- Walnuts
- Wine, dry white

# PENNE WITH SMOKED SHIITAKE AND RADICCHIO

Serves 3 to 4

Vegetarian

Alder or applewood wood chips, for smoking

5 ounces sliced shiitake mushrooms (about 2 1/2 cups)

2 tablespoons extra-virgin olive oil, plus more as needed

1 large shallot, julienned

1/2 teaspoon kosher salt, plus more as needed

12 ounces (1 small head) radicchio, trimmed and chopped into 2 × 1/2-inch pieces

1/4 cup heavy cream

1/3 cup grated Parmesan cheese, plus more for serving

12 ounces penne pasta

Freshly ground black pepper

Smoked shiitake take the place of pancetta in this vegetarian version of an Italian classic. Penne works nicely in this dish, and another good choice would be fusilli or a long, somewhat wide pasta like tagliatelle or fettuccine.

Add alder or applewood chips to a smoking skillet (see page 20) and heat over high until the chips are smoking. Place the mushrooms on the rack, cover, and smoke for no more than 2 minutes. Remove the mushrooms from the skillet and set aside.

Heat the olive oil in a large saucepan over medium heat. Add the shallot and sauté for 2 to 3 minutes, or until softened. Add the smoked shiitake, sprinkle with the salt, and cook for 7 to 8 minutes, stirring occasionally until lightly browned. Stir in the radicchio and cook for 5 to 6 minutes, or until wilted and darkened. Stir in the cream and cheese. Cover and set aside.

Bring a large pot of lightly salted water to a boil over medium-high heat. Add the penne and cook for 7 to 10 minutes, or until al dente. Drain, reserving 1/2 cup of the cooking water.

Add the cooked pasta to the mushroom mixture in the pan along with the reserved cooking water. Toss until combined and creamy. Taste, and season with additional salt and pepper if needed. Serve immediately with additional grated Parmesan cheese.

# "SPICY-YAKI" MUSHROOM JERKY

Makes 18 to 20 pieces

Vegan

1 tablespoon virgin coconut oil

2 ¹/₂ tablespoons brown sugar

¹/₄ cup smoked shoyu, tamari, or low-sodium soy sauce

¹/₂ teaspoon grated peeled fresh ginger

1 teaspoon toasted sesame oil

1 teaspoon fresh lemon juice

¹/₄ teaspoon Chinese five-spice powder

Pinch of red pepper flakes

¹/₄ cup water

8 ounces shiitake mushrooms, stemmed (about 4 cups)

Sesame seeds, for garnish (optional)

Try this sweet, a little spicy, and healthy, chewy, delicious snack. Shiitakes are the preferred mushroom for jerky; they absorb the marinade well and overall have the best consistency after cooking. You can use other mushrooms, such as king trumpets, oyster, or portobello, but you may need to adjust the cooking time. The mushrooms shrink quite a bit (up to 50 percent), so double or triple the marinade for a larger batch.

In a small saucepan over medium-high heat, combine the coconut oil, brown sugar, smoked shoyu, ginger, sesame oil, lemon juice, five-spice powder, pepper flakes, and the water and bring to a simmer. Simmer for 2 to 3 minutes. Remove the pan from the heat, stir in the mushrooms, and toss until well coated. Let cool. Place the mushrooms and the marinade in a sealed plastic bag and refrigerate for at least 4 hours or overnight.

Preheat a convection oven (the ideal choice) to 210 degrees F, or standard oven to 235 degrees F. Line a baking sheet with parchment paper.

Drain the mushrooms, (reserve the marinade for another batch if you like) spread them out evenly on the prepared baking sheet and sprinkle with sesame seeds (if using). Bake for about 3 hours, turning once or twice during baking time, until the mushrooms are tender, chewy, and a little dried around the edges. Let cool and enjoy. Store leftovers in an airtight container in the refrigerator for 3 to 4 days.

# SESAME AND CHILI-ROASTED SHIITAKE WITH GARLIC FRIED RICE

Serves 2 to 3

Vegetarian with vegan option

## GARLIC FRIED RICE

1½ tablespoons grapeseed oil
  or vegetable oil

1½ tablespoons minced garlic

3 cups cooked long-grain rice

Kosher salt

## ROASTED SHIITAKE

1 teaspoon sesame oil

1 tablespoon white miso paste

2 tablespoons low-sodium
  tamari

1½ teaspoons honey or agave
  syrup

1 tablespoon Sichuan spicy
  chili crisp (available in most
  grocery stores)

¼ cup grapeseed oil or
  canola oil

10 to 12 shiitake mushroom caps

## FOR SERVING

Toasted sesame seeds

Thinly sliced green onions

Sesame and soy are a popular combination with shiitake, and although you could use other mushrooms in this dish, shiitakes are a top pick. The spicy chili crisp adds a little crunch and added garlicky umaminess. Roasting the mushrooms after a brief soak in the marinade elevates an already delicious combination of flavors. Garlic fried rice also makes a terrific side dish for chicken or fish. You may cook the rice a day ahead or use leftover white rice if you happen to have any on hand—day-old rice cooks up beautifully when fried.

---

**TO MAKE THE GARLIC FRIED RICE,** heat the oil in a wok or large skillet over high heat. Stir in the garlic and cook for 1 to 2 minutes until golden. Add the cooked rice and toss quickly in the hot oil to thoroughly warm and coat. Let the rice sit undisturbed in the hot pan, for 2 to 3 minutes, or until crispy on the bottom. Toss again. Taste and add salt as needed. Transfer the rice to a bowl.

Preheat the oven to 400 degrees F.

**TO MAKE THE ROASTED SHIITAKE,** in a medium bowl, whisk together the sesame oil, miso paste, tamari, honey, spicy chili crisp, and grapeseed oil. Add the mushroom caps and gently toss until well coated. Spread out the mushrooms on a nonstick baking sheet, cap sides up, and roast for 5 to 6 minutes, or until tender and lightly browned.

**TO SERVE,** divide the garlic rice among serving plates and top with the mushrooms. Garnish with sesame seeds and green onions.

# BAKED CORN AND CHEDDAR GRITS WITH WILD MUSHROOM RAGU

### GRITS

2 tablespoons butter, plus more
  for the baking dish

1 cup fresh or thawed frozen
  corn kernels

1 1/2 cups whole milk

2 cups water

1 cup stone-ground grits

1 teaspoon kosher salt, plus
  more as needed

Freshly ground black pepper

1 1/4 cups grated aged cheddar
  cheese, divided

2 tablespoons minced fresh
  chives

2 eggs

Fresh corn and aged cheddar add a little something extra to these delicious baked grits. Corn and shiitake mushrooms go especially well together. Chanterelles, oysters, or cremini would also be good choices. Mix and match if you like. I urge you to use stone-ground grits if you can find them, if not, regular grits will do.

Preheat the oven to 350 degrees F and butter a 9 × 9-inch casserole dish.

**TO MAKE THE GRITS,** in a blender, combine the corn and milk and blend until almost smooth; there will be small flecks of corn in the milk.

Transfer the milk mixture into a medium covered saucepan, add the water, and bring to a boil over medium-high heat. Whisk in the grits with the salt and a few turns of pepper. Turn the heat to medium-low, and simmer, whisking or stirring constantly, for about 5 minutes, or

## MUSHROOM RAGU

2 strips thick-cut bacon, cut crosswise into 1/4-inch slices

1 large shallot, thinly sliced

2 tablespoons butter, divided

1 tablespoon olive oil

8 ounces shiitake, oyster, chanterelle, or cremini mushrooms, trimmed and roughly chopped (about 4 cups)

Pinch of kosher salt, plus more as needed

1/2 cup red wine

2 cups Roasted Mushroom Stock (page 232)

2 thyme sprigs

2 tablespoons cornstarch

1/4 cup water

Freshly ground black pepper

## OPTIONAL TOPPINGS

Microgreens

Fresh parsley

Shaved cheddar cheese

until the grits are smooth and just beginning to thicken. Cover, turn the heat to low, and gently simmer, stirring occasionally, for 20 to 25 minutes, or until the grits are softened and fully cooked. Stir in 3/4 cup of the cheese, the butter, and chives. Taste and adjust the seasoning with additional salt and pepper if needed. Remove from the heat and let cool for about 10 minutes.

In a bowl, vigorously whisk the eggs until foamy and fold them into the grits. Pour the mixture into the casserole dish and top with the remaining 1/2 cup cheese. Bake for 35 to 45 minutes, or until the grits are set and the cheese is lightly browned.

**TO MAKE THE RAGU,** in a medium skillet over medium heat, cook the bacon lardons for 5 to 6 minutes, or until crispy. Transfer the bacon to a plate.

Drain all but about 1 teaspoon of the bacon fat from the skillet. Add the shallot and sauté for 2 to 3 minutes, or until softened. Transfer the shallot to the plate with the bacon.

In the same skillet, raise the heat to medium-high and add 1 tablespoon of the butter and the olive oil. When the butter is foaming, add the mushrooms, toss to coat, and sauté, adding a pinch of salt as the mushrooms begin to color. Cook for 5 to 7 minutes, or until the mushrooms are golden and cooked through. Add the wine, cook until it's mostly absorbed, pour in the stock, add the thyme sprigs, and turn the heat to medium-low. Simmer for 10 to 15 minutes, or until the stock has reduced by about one-third in amount.

Whisk the cornstarch together with the water, add to the ragu, and continue to simmer for 3 to 5 minutes, or until the ragu has thickened. Whisk in the remaining tablespoon of butter, taste, adjust the seasoning as needed with salt and pepper, and remove from the heat.

**TO SERVE,** place a spoonful of grits on each plate. Add a helping of the mushrooms and drizzle with the sauce. Top with a sprinkle of microgreens or parsley and shavings of cheddar cheese.

# SHIITAKE AND SHRIMP WONTONS WITH SWEET PEPPER STIR-FRY AND GINGER-LIME DRESSING

Serves 4

**GINGER-LIME DRESSING**

½ shallot, minced

1 teaspoon grated peeled fresh
   ginger

Grated zest and juice of 1 lime

1 garlic clove, minced

2 tablespoons rice vinegar

2 tablespoons tamari or
   low-sodium soy sauce

2 tablespoons mirin

1 teaspoon sesame oil

1 teaspoon honey

½ cup mayonnaise (preferably
   Japanese Kewpie)

A few drops of chili oil

**SHIITAKE AND SHRIMP
WONTONS**

4 ounces fresh shiitake mushrooms, stemmed (freeze
   and reserve for stock; about
   2 cups)

Who doesn't love a crispy wonton? These flavorful fried wontons are filled with shrimp, shiitake mushrooms, water chestnuts, and chili crisp, served over a crisp, sweet pepper stir-fry and drizzled with a gingery lime and honey dressing. Enjoy as an appetizer or light lunch.

---

**TO MAKE THE DRESSING,** in a small bowl, whisk together the shallot, ginger, lime zest and juice, garlic, vinegar, tamari, mirin, sesame oil, honey, and mayonnaise. Add the chili oil to taste.

Preheat the oven to the warm setting. Line a plate with paper towels.

**TO MAKE THE WONTONS,** mince the shiitake by hand or in a food processor and transfer to a bowl.

2 tablespoons grapeseed or vegetable oil

3 green onions, minced white parts (reserve the green parts for the stir-fry)

1 tablespoon chili crisp

1 1/2 tablespoons tamari or low-sodium soy sauce

2 tablespoons hoisin sauce

1/3 cup water chestnuts, minced

4 ounces (about 8 large) raw shrimp, peeled and deveined

1/2 teaspoon kosher salt, plus more as needed

1 egg

1 tablespoon water

24 wonton wrappers

Neutral oil, for frying

**SWEET PEPPER STIR-FRY**

1 tablespoon grapeseed oil or vegetable oil

1/2 teaspoon sesame oil

1 red bell pepper, seeded and julienned

1 cup mung bean sprouts

1 medium carrot, julienned

Reserved green parts of the green onions, sliced into 2-inch pieces

Chopped fresh cilantro, for garnish

Microgreens, for garnish

Heat the grapeseed oil in a medium skillet over medium heat. Add the shiitake and cook, stirring often, until cooked through, dry, and caramelized, 3 to 4 minutes. Stir in the green onions and cook for 1 to 2 minutes, or until softened. Add the chili crisp, tamari, hoisin, and water chestnuts and mix well. Transfer to a bowl and set aside.

Place the shrimp in the food processor and process until minced. Add them to the bowl with the mushroom mixture, add the salt, and mix thoroughly. (Cook a teaspoon of the mixture in a skillet over medium heat and taste for additional seasoning.)

Mix the egg and water together in a small bowl.

Lay out 1 wonton wrapper, diagonally facing you. Place 1 teaspoon of the mushroom mixture in the middle and to the left of center. Using your finger or a brush, lightly coat the egg wash along the outside edges of the wrapper. Fold the wrapper in half over the filling, making a triangle shape, then firmly press the edges down to seal. Transfer to a plate and repeat with the remaining wrappers and filling.

Heat 2 inches of neutral oil in a heavy, deep saucepan over medium-high heat to 340 degrees F. Fry the wontons, a few at a time, for 2 to 3 minutes, or until crispy and golden brown. Transfer them to the paper towel-lined plate to drain. Lightly season with salt. Keep in the warm oven until ready to serve.

**TO MAKE THE STIR-FRY,** heat the grapeseed oil and sesame oil in a medium skillet over high heat. Stir in the bell pepper, bean sprouts, carrot, and the green onion and quickly cook, stirring often, for 1 to 2 minutes. The vegetables should still be crispy. Remove from the pan.

**TO SERVE,** divide the stir-fry among four plates. Arrange the wontons over the stir-fry, drizzle with the dressing, and top with a sprinkling of microgreens and cilantro.

# SHIITAKE PÂTÉ WITH WONTON SESAME CRISPS

Serves 2 to 3 as an appetizer

Vegetarian

1/4 cup walnut pieces

1/2 cup milk

2 tablespoons butter, divided

1 large shallot minced, or
   2 tablespoons minced red
   onion

1 large garlic clove, minced

1 tablespoon grapeseed oil or
   canola oil

4 ounces roughly chopped shiitake mushrooms, stemmed
   (about 2 cups)

1/2 teaspoon salt, plus more as
   needed

2 tablespoons dry sherry

1 tablespoon soy sauce

3 tablespoons heavy cream

1 tablespoon chopped fresh
   parsley leaves

Freshly ground black pepper

Consider this earthy mushroom pâté a simple yet decadent pleasure. You'll love it as an appetizer with the Wonton Crisps (opposite) or enjoy as part of a charcuterie board with pickled vegetables or on a toasted baguette. Soaking the walnuts in milk reduces their bitterness and adds a creamy texture and added nutty flavor.

---

Soak the walnuts in the milk for at least 30 minutes, up to overnight (refrigerated). Drain and set aside.

Heat 1 tablespoon of butter in a medium saucepan over medium-low heat. Add the shallot and garlic and sauté for 2 to 3 minutes, or until softened.

Raise the heat to medium-high and add the remaining 1 tablespoon of butter and the grapeseed oil to the pan. Add the mushrooms and sauté for 5 to 7 minutes, salting halfway through cooking time, until the mushrooms are cooked through and golden. Stir in the sherry and stir for 1 to 2 minutes until absorbed. Remove the pan from the heat and let cool.

Transfer the mixture to a blender, add the walnuts, soy sauce, cream, and parsley, and process until smooth. Taste and season with salt and pepper.

# WONTON SESAME CRISPS

Makes 48 wonton crisps

Vegetarian

**24 wonton wrappers**

**Sesame seeds (black, white, or both), for sprinkling**

**Sea salt**

These are so easy; you'll want to make extra for snacking. Spraying the wontons with a light mist of water before adding the sesame seeds helps them adhere to the crisps.

Preheat the oven to 400 degrees F. Spray a nonstick baking sheet with cooking oil spray.

Using a sharp knife, cut the wonton wrappers in half diagonally to make 2 triangle-shaped pieces of each wonton.

Lay the wrappers in a single layer on the baking sheet, using a spray bottle, spray the wrappers evenly with a light mist of water, sprinkle them with sesame seeds, then spray again with cooking oil spray. Bake until lightly golden, 4 to 5 minutes. Remove from the oven and sprinkle lightly with sea salt.

Once cooled, the crisps can be kept in an airtight container at room temperature for up to 1 week.

# TRUFFLE

**TRUFFLES** are deliciously edible fungi, filled with spores like mushrooms, but that grow underground. Not exactly a mushroom, but a close cousin, the truffle rightly earns a mention in every culinary mushroom book.

Truffles are symbiotic and attach to the roots of oak or hazelnut trees through their mycelium and are influenced by their flavorful essence. Although initially found in Italy and France, they are now cultivated worldwide. Of the over 200 truffle varieties, only a few are famous for their culinary qualities, including the ones following.

## WINTER BLACK TRUFFLE *Tuber melanosporum*

Probably the most famous truffle, also known as Périgord, winter blacks are in season from mid-November through March. These iconic truffles are renowned and revered for their intense flavor and aroma, with earthy undertones of Cognac and chocolate. Gentle heating amplifies the aroma, but be careful never to cook them at high heat, or the flavor will disappear. Serve with eggs, rice, and pasta dishes or simply shave on good, buttered bread with a sprinkle of fleur de sel.

## SUMMER BLACK TRUFFLE *Tuber aestivum*

Summer black truffles lack the intense aroma of their more expensive cousins, the winter black truffles. However, their mild nutty flavor makes them versatile in culinary use and they are more affordable. They appear in late spring and are in season through early fall. They are best served warm, shaved generously in pasta dishes, or tucked under the skin of roasted duck or chicken.

## BURGUNDY TRUFFLE *Tuber uncinatum*

These powerfully pungent, versatile, and highly regarded truffles are considered the gems of the autumn season. They have a rich earthy flavor and an aroma redolent of roasted hazelnuts. Burgundy truffles are often added to olive oil for dressings and infused into butters or honey.

## WINTER WHITE TRUFFLE *Tuber magnatum pico*

The winter white truffle is considered the king of truffles and is found during late fall through early winter to the joy of mushroom enthusiasts and avid culinarians. It's a very expensive truffle, but luckily a little goes a long way. Unlike more robust truffle varieties, white truffles should always be enjoyed raw and freshly shaved directly onto a warm finished dish. This radiant heat is all that is needed to bring out the mushroom's sublime, aromatic presence.

## SUMMER WHITE TRUFFLE *Tuber magnatum pico*

The summer white truffle is the same variety as the winter white truffle and is available from mid-January through the end of April. Although not quite as flavorful as the winter variety, it is still a delicious ingredient, with a musky, earthy fragrance and sweet, mild garlicky flavor. It pairs nicely with spring dishes, vegetables, and greens.

## TRUFFLE TIPS

- Avoid rinsing truffles; instead, lightly brush off any dirt. Fresh truffles will keep in the refrigerator for 1 to 2 weeks, wrapped individually in paper towels, and stored in an airtight container.
- For longer storage, freeze black truffles for up to 4 months. Place them, unwashed and vacuum-packed, in the freezer. Grate while still frozen directly onto your dish.
- Use a truffle slicer, mandoline, or a very sharp knife for serving truffles.
- Add leftover truffle shavings to room temperature butter or mix with sea salt to add decadent truffle essence to your dishes.

# MUSHROOM MEDLEYS

**BECAUSE SOMETIMES** more is better—especially when it comes to mushrooms! These recipes encourage using a mixture of mushrooms. This is a place where three is not a crowd; it's just about tasting delicious!

# WILD MUSHROOM SAUCE WITH RED WINE AND GORGONZOLA

Makes about 2 cups

Vegetarian

1 tablespoon olive oil

1 tablespoon butter

8 ounces mixed mushrooms; wild and/or cultivated, such as shiitake, chanterelle, hedgehog, oyster, cremini, or portobello, cleaned, trimmed, and sliced (about 4 cups)

$\frac{1}{3}$ cup Merlot or Syrah

1 tablespoon low-sodium soy sauce

$\frac{1}{4}$ cup heavy cream

Kosher salt

Freshly ground black pepper

Grilled steak or grilled slices of bread, for serving

Crumbled Gorgonzola or another mild blue cheese of choice, for serving

Chopped fresh parsley or thyme sprigs, for garnish

This is the ultimate mushroom steak topping. It's brimming with rich wine flavor and is a cinch to make. Add crumbled, soft blue cheese, pop under the broiler before serving, and sprinkle with chopped fresh parsley for a finishing touch. Choose a nice bottle of wine for including in the recipe and don't let the rest go to waste!

Heat the olive oil and butter in a medium skillet over medium-high heat. Add the mushrooms and sear for 6 to 7 minutes, turning occasionally, until the mushrooms are tender and deeply golden. Pour in the wine and cook, stirring often, until the liquid is reduced by half. Lower the heat to medium, add the soy sauce and cream, and simmer, for 3 to 4 minutes, or until the sauce has thickened. Taste, and season with salt and pepper. Serve immediately over grilled steak or slices of grilled bread topped with blue cheese and chopped fresh parsley.

# CREAMY WILD RICE AND MUSHROOM SOUP

Serves 6

Vegetarian

½ cup wild rice blend

4 tablespoons butter or olive oil, divided

12 ounces fresh mushrooms, cleaned, trimmed, and chopped (about 6 cups)

1 teaspoon kosher salt, plus more as needed

½ small sweet onion, finely chopped

1 medium leek, white and light green parts only, quartered, cleaned, and cut crosswise into ⅛-inch-thick half-moon slices

1 celery stalk, finely chopped

1 carrot, finely chopped

2 garlic cloves, minced

2 tablespoons all-purpose flour

4 cups Roasted Mushroom Stock (page 232), or chicken or vegetable stock, plus more as needed

1 cup half-and-half or whole milk

2 or 3 thyme sprigs

2 bay leaves

1 (2 × 3-inch) piece Parmesan rind

Freshly ground black pepper

2 tablespoons chopped fresh parsley

Splash of fresh lemon juice or medium-dry sherry (optional)

This creamy, cool weather, blended wild rice and mushroom soup is as heartwarming as it sounds. The combination of leek and sweet onion adds a double layer of savory allium flavor. Most any mushroom will work well in this soup, though a variety of mushrooms may be even better. You'll find wild rice blends (usually a mixture of wild, white, red, and brown rice) at your local supermarket. This soup just calls for toasted crusty bread slices and a buttery glass of Chardonnay.

Prepare the rice blend according to the package instructions. Set aside.

Heat 2 tablespoons of butter in a large Dutch oven or pot over medium-high heat. Add the mushrooms and sauté, lightly seasoning them with salt halfway through, until cooked and golden brown, 7 to 8 minutes. Transfer the mushrooms to a plate.

Lower the heat to medium, add the remaining 2 tablespoons of butter and sauté the onion, leek, celery, and carrot for 5 to 6 minutes, or until well softened. Add the garlic and cook, stirring often, for another 1 to 2 minutes (do not brown).

Add the flour and stir for 1 to 2 minutes until the vegetables are well coated. Pour in the stock and the half-and-half, stir, then add the thyme sprigs, bay leaves, and Parmesan rind. Stir in the cooked rice, and bring to a simmer.

Turn the heat to medium-low and simmer for 20 to 25 minutes, or until the soup has thickened and the vegetables are tender. Taste along the way, adjusting with additional salt and pepper. Add a splash of stock or water if the soup is too thick. Remove the thyme sprigs, bay leaves, and Parmesan rind. Stir in the parsley and finish with a splash of lemon juice or sherry (if using).

# SLOW-COOKED MUSHROOMS

Serves 4 as a side dish

Vegan

1 pound whole white button,
   cremini, hedgehog, or
   pioppino mushrooms (or
   a mixture), cleaned and
   trimmed, larger mushrooms
   halved (6 to 8 cups)
6 garlic cloves, sliced
1 1/2 tablespoons olive oil
Kosher salt
Freshly ground black pepper

This recipe, adapted from one by well-known cookbook author Paula Wolfert, is definitely worth passing along. Slow cooking results in tender mushrooms with concentrated flavor and a welcome hands-off technique. Dense, hearty mushrooms work well in this dish. You will love these straight from the pot.

To take these mushrooms to the next level, skip the final seasoning, and add the cooked mushrooms to a hot skillet with a generous amount of butter and toss until golden. Finish with a splash of lemon juice and a healthy sprinkle of coarse salt, ground black pepper, and fresh parsley. Wonderful on toasted crusty bread or served as a side with roast chicken or steak.

In a heavy 1-quart pot or Dutch oven, combine the mushrooms, garlic, and olive oil and toss until well coated.

Place a sheet of parchment paper directly on top of the mushroom mixture, cover with the lid, and cook over low heat, shaking the pot occasionally to ensure even cooking, for 45 to 55 minutes. Taste, and season with salt and pepper.

# WILD MUSHROOM BREAD PUDDING WITH MANCHEGO, SERRANO HAM, AND SHERRY

Serves 4 to 6

2 tablespoons butter, divided,
    plus more as needed
6 ounces brioche or challah
    bread, cut into 1-inch cubes
    (about 4 cups)
2 tablespoons olive oil, divided,
    plus more as needed
½ onion, finely chopped
½ fennel bulb, cored, and finely
    chopped
Kosher salt, plus ½ teaspoon,
    divided
2 medium garlic cloves, minced
4 ounces thinly sliced Serrano
    ham, chopped
4 ounces fresh mushrooms,
    cleaned, trimmed, and
    roughly chopped (about
    2 cups)
2 tablespoons medium-dry
    sherry, Amontillado if
    available
3 eggs
1½ cups half-and-half
⅛ teaspoon ground nutmeg
¼ teaspoon smoked paprika
1 cup grated Manchego cheese,
    divided
Freshly ground black pepper
2 tablespoons finely chopped
    fresh parsley

The classic combination of woodsy mushrooms and Spanish sherry marry with Serrano ham and Manchego cheese to add a Spanish twist to this flavorful bread pudding. A mixture of wild and/or cultivated mushrooms, such as porcini, oyster, cremini, shiitake, trumpet, or hedgehog would all be good choices. Be sure to remove any tough ends of the mushroom stems before cooking.

Amontillado is a unique and complex medium-dry sherry; you will likely find a bottle at your local wine store. Offer a glass to your guests before dinner as an aperitif.

Preheat the oven to 350 degrees F. Butter a 1½-quart casserole or gratin dish.

Spread the cubed bread on a baking sheet and toast for about 15 minutes, or until dried. Remove from the oven and set aside.

Heat 1 tablespoon of butter and 1 tablespoon of olive oil in a large skillet over medium heat. Add the onion, fennel, and a pinch of salt and cook for 5 to 6 minutes, or until the onion and fennel begin to soften and caramelize. Add the garlic and cook for another minute. Transfer the mixture to a bowl.

Raise the heat to medium-high, add the remaining 1 tablespoon of butter and 1 tablespoon of olive oil. When the oil is hot, sear the ham until crispy, then add the mushrooms and sauté for 7 to 8 minutes adding a pinch of salt as the mushrooms begin to color. Add more butter or oil if necessary. Stir in the sherry and cook for 2 to 3 minutes, or until all of the liquid is reduced to a glaze. Remove the pan from the heat.

In a medium bowl, whisk together the eggs, half-and-half, nutmeg, and paprika. Add $^3/_4$ cup of Manchego cheese, $^1/_2$ teaspoon salt, 2 to 3 grinds of freshly ground black pepper and stir until well combined.

Fold the dried bread cubes and the mushroom mixture into the custard, coating the bread well with the liquid. (To taste for seasoning, pan-fry a tiny spoonful of the mixture and adjust the seasoning before proceeding.)

Transfer the mixture to the prepared baking dish. Press the bread down into the custard and smooth the surface a little. Sprinkle the remaining $^1/_4$ cup of Manchego cheese over the top.

Bake for 30 to 45 minutes, or until the top is golden brown and the custard is set. The baking time will depend on the depth of your chosen baking dish. Sprinkle with parsley and serve.

Leftovers can be tightly covered and refrigerated for up to 3 days.

# HERB-ROASTED MUSHROOM ALFREDO

Serves 3 to 4

Vegetarian

1 pound assorted mushrooms, cleaned, stemmed, and thickly sliced (about 7 cups)

3 tablespoons olive oil

2 teaspoons kosher salt, plus more as needed

¼ teaspoon freshly ground black pepper, plus more as needed

Handful fresh hearty herbs, such as rosemary, thyme, or sage

12 ounces long pasta, such as fettuccine, tagliatelle, or spaghetti

2 tablespoons butter

1 small garlic clove, grated

1½ cups heavy cream or half-and-half

1 egg yolk

1 cup grated Parmesan cheese

The mushrooms in this recipe absorb a layer of concentrated herby flavor beyond just plain roasting. Assorted cultivated mushrooms are cooked in the oven over a bed of fresh herbs, then lightly simmered in a creamy Alfredo sauce. For this dish I used shiitake and oyster mushrooms. Cremini or even large buttons would also work well, but feel free to choose your favorite. Serve over long pasta, either fresh or dried.

Preheat the oven to 375 degrees F.

In a large bowl, toss together the mushrooms, olive oil, salt, and pepper. Scatter the herbs in a baking pan with a fitted rack. Set the rack over the herbs and spread the mushrooms on the rack. Roast for 18 to 20 minutes, or until golden brown. Let cool, roughly chop the mushrooms, and set aside.

Bring a large pot of lightly salted water to a boil over medium-high heat. Add the pasta and cook for 6 to 8 minutes, or until al dente. Drain, reserving ½ cup of cooking water.

Melt the butter in an extra-large skillet over medium heat. Add the garlic and cook for 1 to 2 minutes, stirring often, until just lightly golden.

Turn the heat to medium-low. Whisk in the cream and egg yolk until smooth. Stir in the mushrooms and 1 heaping teaspoon of the crushed roasted herb leaves (no stems) and simmer gently for 4 to 5 minutes, or until the mushrooms are tender and the sauce is thick and creamy. Taste, and adjust the seasoning with salt and pepper.

Add the pasta, toss to coat with the sauce, and cook for an additional 2 to 3 minutes, adding the reserved pasta water as necessary, until the sauce is creamy and clinging to the pasta. Stir in the cheese and serve immediately.

# WILD MUSHROOM ARANCINI
# WITH SMOKED SCAMORZA

Makes 18 to 20 arancini

Vegetarian option

4 cups low-sodium chicken or
   vegetable stock

¼ ounce dried porcini

2 tablespoons butter

½ small onion, minced

¼ cup finely diced ham,
   prosciutto, or pancetta
   (optional)

2 to 3 ounces wild mushrooms,
   cleaned, trimmed, and
   minced (about 1 cup)

Pinch of kosher salt, plus ½
   teaspoons salt, divided, plus
   more as needed

1 cup carnaroli or Arborio rice,
   pulsed once or twice in a food
   processor

⅓ cup white wine

Freshly ground black pepper

3 tablespoons grated Parmesan
   cheese

1 tablespoon minced fresh
   parsley

4 ounces smoked scamorza or
   smoked mozzarella cut into
   ⅓-inch cubes

2 large eggs

2 tablespoons water

1 cup all-purpose flour

1½ cups Italian breadcrumbs
   or panko breadcrumbs
   (for panko, pulse in a food
   processor for a finer crumb)

Peanut or vegetable oil, for
   frying

Marinara sauce of choice, for
   serving

Arancini, a popular Sicilian street food, are Italian rice balls often made with leftover risotto. Filled with meat or cheese, coated in breadcrumbs and fried, arancini are a staple of Sicilian cuisine, and no wonder! Some Italians feel Arborio rice is a little large for arancini, so a short-grain specialty arancini rice is available in Italy made just for these beloved Sicilian snacks. You will find it online or possibly in your local Italian market. By pulsing regular uncooked Arborio or carnaroli rice a couple of times in the food processor before cooking, you can easily make your own. Smaller grains like these are also ideal for making risotto for stuffing morels. Smoked scamorza may be difficult to find, so feel free to substitute with a good whole-milk smoked mozzarella.

Combine the stock and dried porcini in a medium saucepan over medium heat and gently simmer for about 20 minutes. Strain the stock, return it to the saucepan, and place over low heat. Finely chop the mushrooms and set aside.

Melt the butter in another medium saucepan or deep skillet over medium-low heat. Add the onion and sauté for about 3 minutes, until softened. Stir in the ham and cook for an additional 1 to 2 minutes. Raise the heat to medium-high, stir in the fresh and reserved rehydrated mushrooms, and pinch of salt. Cook for 3 to 4 minutes, stirring often, until the mushroom mixture is dry and a deep golden color. Add the rice and cook for about 2 minutes, stirring often, until the rice is translucent. Pour in the wine, stir, and cook briefly until the liquid is reduced and almost dry.

Begin adding the reserved stock, 1 ladleful at a time, stirring constantly, adding more only when the liquid is absorbed. Continue to add stock, stirring continuously for 25 to 30 minutes, or until the rice is soft with a very slight bite in the center. Taste and adjust the seasoning with salt and pepper. Remove from the heat, spread on a baking sheet, and chill for 1 to 2 hours. At this point the rice can be covered and refrigerated overnight.

When the rice is cool, stir in the Parmesan cheese and parsley. Using a spoon or 2-inch scoop, form the mixture into 1 1/2 × 2-inch balls, tucking a piece of scamorza into the center of each ball.

Line a baking sheet with parchment paper. In a small bowl, whisk together the eggs and water. Season the flour with 1/2 teaspoon salt. Place the flour and breadcrumbs separately into two shallow bowls.

Dip each rice ball into the flour, then the egg wash, then roll and evenly coat with the breadcrumbs. Set them aside on the prepared baking sheet. Fill a deep saucepan or pot with 2 inches of oil over medium heat and bring the oil to 350 degrees F. Add the rice balls to the oil with a spider or slotted spoon, and fry, turning gently, until the rice balls are golden, about 6 minutes. Transfer to a rack or paper towels to drain and sprinkle lightly with salt. Serve with marinara sauce for dipping.

# FLAVORFUL STOCKS and broths are the substance and backbone of any successful savory creation. First, a quick definition:

**Stocks**: Stocks are simmered for a long time, often with bones and vegetables that are pre-roasted. It generally has a deep, intense flavor.

**Broths**: Broths are cooked for less time than a stock, and the vegetables or meats are not roasted. The flavor is less intense than a stock.

Stocks and broths are indispensable components for producing fantastic dishes. Easy to make, they require little preparation and mostly hands-off time for the cooking, requiring only a quick skim every hour or so. Stocks and broths can be refrigerated for up to 1 week or frozen in airtight containers or ice cube trays for several months, so you'll have flavorful, invaluable stock waiting for you whenever you need it.

Let your creative inner chef decide its fate. Do you prefer a deep intense stock? Simmer it longer and add more ingredients. Don't be afraid to try different vegetables—this is a good time to use what's been ignored in your produce bin. And be sure to taste along the way.

Here are a few suggestions for making almost any type of stock:
- Start with cool or cold liquid. Cold water slowly draws out the flavors of the ingredients and helps keep the stock clear and not cloudy.
- Use salt minimally! Do not add salt until after the stock has finished cooking. The stock will reduce in volume as it cooks. A better idea is to not salt at all and add salt to the resulting dish you make with the stock.
- Balance the ingredient-to-water ratio to include at least one-half ingredients (vegetables and/or meats) to water. The higher proportion of ingredients, the more flavorful the stock.
- Do not boil. Boiling makes for stock cloudy, as the fats and impurities will incorporate into the liquid instead of floating to the surface, where they can be skimmed off. Keep the broth or stock at a steady simmer and try not to stir it.
- For a clear stock, let the stock or broth strain naturally. When straining, avoid pressing on the ingredients in the sieve.

# QUICK MUSHROOM BROTH

⅛ ounce dried mushrooms, of choice (5 or 6 pieces)

3 cups water

This is a fast and easy light broth that will add a little extra mushroom flavor to your dish without a lot of effort. Use it to cook vegetables or add it to sauces. Be creative and use a combination of dried mushrooms you may have in your pantry. Porcini and shiitake are both good choices for umami-rich broths, or use lobster mushrooms for a seafood-flavored broth. Make sure to use a fine-mesh strainer to remove any residual dirt from the dried mushrooms.

In a medium saucepan over medium-low heat, combine the dried mushrooms and water and bring to a simmer. Cook for 20 minutes, or until the broth reaches your desired flavor.

Strain through a fine-mesh strainer and cool.

The broth can be stored in airtight containers or sealable freezer bags in the refrigerator for up to 1 week or frozen for up to 3 months.

# MUSHROOM BROTH

Makes about 2 1/2 quarts

Vegan

1 gallon cold water

1 sweet onion, peeled and
   quartered

6 to 8 garlic cloves

8 ounces fresh button or
   cremini mushrooms, roughly
   chopped (about 4 cups)

1 cup dried mushrooms, such as
   porcini or shiitake, though any
   dried flavorful variety will do

3 or 4 parsley sprigs

2 or 3 thyme sprigs

This light and versatile mushroom broth can be used as a base for soups and consommés.

Fill a large pot with the water. Add the onion, garlic, fresh mushrooms, dried mushrooms, parsley, and thyme and bring to a boil over medium-high heat. Turn the heat to medium-low and maintain a simmer, skimming off any foam that rises to the top, for about 1 1/2 hours, or until the broth reaches your desired flavor. Strain through a fine-mesh strainer and cool.

Store in airtight containers or sealable freezer bags in the refrigerator for up to 1 week or freeze for up to 3 months.

# MUSHROOM DASHI

Makes 4 cups

Vegan

6 dried donko shiitake
   mushrooms

4 cups water

A stock fundamental in Japanese cuisine, this umami-filled mushroom dashi makes a flavorful base for miso, noodle, and clear broth soups. Simmer with one sheet of dried kombu for a more intense broth, then add tofu, mushrooms, and chopped vegetables for a filling nutritious soup.

Soak the shiitake in the water for several hours or overnight in the refrigerator. When the mushrooms have softened, squeeze to drain, and reserve the liquid. Cut away the stems and discard. Strain the soaking water through a fine-mesh strainer.

Although best fresh, dashi can be stored in airtight containers in the refrigerator for up to 1 week or frozen for up to 1 month.

# ROASTED MUSHROOM STOCK AND DEMI-GLACE

Makes 2 quarts

Vegan

1¹⁄₂ pounds fresh mushrooms, such as button, cremini, or shiitake (10 to 12 cups)

¹⁄₂ ounce dried shiitake and/or porcini mushrooms (about ¹⁄₂ cup)

1 celery stalk, roughly chopped

1 medium carrot, roughly chopped

1 small onion, roughly chopped

1 leek, white and light green parts only, cleaned and roughly chopped

¹⁄₂ head garlic, separated into cloves

3 tablespoons olive oil

¹⁄₄ cup double-concentrated tomato paste

1 gallon cold water

3 or 4 peppercorns

2 or 3 fresh thyme sprigs

3 or 4 bay leaves

1 cup red wine

You cannot go wrong with this versatile, flavorful mushroom stock. Use it for making gravies, sauces, and hearty soups. Continue to reduce for an hour or two and you'll enjoy a rich demi-glace.

Preheat the oven to 375 degrees F.

In a large bowl, combine the fresh mushrooms, dried mushrooms, celery, carrot, onion, leek, garlic, and olive oil. Toss until well coated and spread out the vegetables on a nonstick baking sheet. Roast for 20 minutes. Remove from the oven, stir in the tomato paste to coat the vegetables, and continue to roast for another 30 minutes, or until all are nicely caramelized.

Fill a large pot with the water and add the peppercorns, thyme sprigs, and bay leaves. Add the roasted vegetables, then add the red wine to the pan drippings, stir to deglaze, and scrape the pan drippings into the pot.

Bring this all to a low simmer over medium-high heat. Turn the heat to medium-low and continue to simmer, skimming off any foam that comes to the top, for 1¹⁄₂ to 2 hours, or until the liquid has reduced by half or to about 2 quarts. Strain and cool.

The stock can then be stored in airtight containers or sealable freezer bags in the refrigerator for up to 1 week or frozen for up to 6 months.

# MUSHROOM DEMI-GLACE

Makes about 2 cups

Vegan

2 quarts Roasted Mushroom
Stock (opposite)

1 tablespoon arrowroot,
cornstarch, potato starch, or
gelatin

2 tablespoons water

Demi-glace is a super-flavorful, concentrated sauce resulting from an hours-long reduction of rich, roasted stock. It's wonderful to have on hand to flavor soups and stews, just a spoonful adds instant umami flavor. If you're using the demi-glace as a sauce, season with salt and pepper. If you're adding it to a soup or sauce, wait and season your finished dish instead.

In a large saucepan over medium- to medium-high heat, simmer the roasted mushroom stock for $1\frac{1}{2}$ to 2 hours until it is reduced to about 2 cups.

In a small bowl, combine the arrowroot with the water and mix until smooth to make a slurry.

Add the slurry to the saucepan and whisk until smooth. Continue to simmer for 5 to 6 minutes, or until the sauce has thickened.

Demi-glace can be stored in airtight containers or sealable freezer bags in the refrigerator for up to 1 week or frozen for up to 6 months.

# LOBSTER MUSHROOM STOCK

Makes 6 to 8 cups

Vegan

2 tablespoons olive oil

1 large onion, quartered

2 large garlic cloves, chopped

Pinch of red pepper flakes

4 celery stalks, roughly chopped

2 carrots, roughly chopped

$1/2$ fennel bulb, roughly chopped

2 tablespoons double-concentrated tomato paste

$2/3$ cup white wine

3 quarts water

$1\frac{1}{2}$ ounces dried lobster mushrooms (about $1\frac{1}{2}$ cups)

3 or 4 parsley sprigs

2 or 3 bay leaves

Kosher salt

This is as close to a lobster stock as you'll find—without the lobster! Add a tablespoon of dried nori or a sheet of kombu toward the end of cooking if you'd like to boost the seafood flavor.

Heat the oil in a large pot over medium heat. Add the onion, garlic, and pepper flakes and cook for about 2 minutes, or until the onion is just translucent. Add the celery, carrots, and fennel and cook for 2 to 3 minutes, or until softened. Add the tomato paste and stir for about 2 minutes, or until the paste has darkened slightly. Stir in the white wine and deglaze the pot, scraping and stirring. Add the water, dried mushrooms, parsley, and bay leaves, raise the heat to medium-high, and bring to a boil. Turn the heat to medium-low and simmer for about $1\frac{1}{2}$ hours, or until the stock is reduced by one-third. If you prefer a more intensely flavored stock, continue to simmer an additional 30 minutes, or until reduced by half. Strain into a bowl. Taste and lightly season with salt as needed.

The stock can be stored in airtight containers or sealable freezer bags in the refrigerator for up to 1 week or frozen for up to 3 months.

# INDEX

## METRIC CONVERSION CHART

| VOLUME MEASUREMENTS | | WEIGHT MEASUREMENTS | | TEMPERATURE CONVERSION | |
|---|---|---|---|---|---|
| U.S. | METRIC | U.S. | METRIC | FAHRENHEIT | CELSIUS |
| 1 teaspoon | 5 ml | ½ ounce | 15 g | 250 | 120 |
| 1 tablespoon | 15 ml | 1 ounce | 30 g | 300 | 150 |
| ¼ cup | 60 ml | 3 ounces | 90 g | 325 | 160 |
| ⅓ cup | 75 ml | 4 ounces | 115 g | 350 | 180 |
| ½ cup | 125 ml | 8 ounces | 225 g | 375 | 190 |
| ⅔ cup | 150 ml | 12 ounces | 350 g | 400 | 200 |
| ¾ cup | 175 ml | 1 pound | 450 g | 425 | 220 |
| 1 cup | 250 ml | 2¼ pounds | 1 kg | 450 | 230 |

# ABOUT THE AUTHOR

**KRISTA TOWNS** is the Wild Epicure editor for *FUNGI Magazine* and the culinary advisor and recipe developer for Circular Farm, a premier mushroom cultivator located in Jackson, South Carolina. She holds a Mushroom Foraging Certification for food service in eighteen states and is an active member of the North American Mycological Association and the South Carolina Upstate Mycological Society. Her culinary training in France helped prepare her as a recipe developer, where she has achieved award-winning success in exclusive chef recipe and cooking competitions.

She provided all of the photography for *Mushroom Gastronomy*. During her career in advertising as an illustrator and designer in Chicago, her work received multiple awards from the New York Society of Illustrators, Communication Arts, and the American Society of Magazine Editors.

Krista enjoys the country life in Aiken, South Carolina, with her husband, John, and their two mischievous spaniels.

Photo credit: Scott Allen Pardue